How to Manage a
Successful
Business
in China

How to Manage a Successful Business in China

Johan Björkstén
Founder of the Chinese PR Agency Eastwei Relations

Anders Hägglund
Former President of Sandvik China

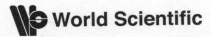 **World Scientific**

NEW JERSEY · LONDON · SINGAPORE · BEIJING · SHANGHAI · HONG KONG · TAIPEI · CHENNAI

Published by

World Scientific Publishing Co. Pte. Ltd.

5 Toh Tuck Link, Singapore 596224

USA office: 27 Warren Street, Suite 401-402, Hackensack, NJ 07601

UK office: 57 Shelton Street, Covent Garden, London WC2H 9HE

British Library Cataloguing-in-Publication Data
A catalogue record for this book is available from the British Library.

ISBN-13 978-981-4287-82-1
ISBN-10 981-4287-82-2

Typeset by Stallion Press
Email: enquiries@stallionpress.com

Printed in Singapore by World Scientific Printers.

Acknowledgements

We would like to thank all of our good friends and business colleagues who have helped provide feedback and input to the manuscript. We are particularly indebted to:

Ernst Behrens, Janine Coughlin, Ian Duffy, Peter Humphrey, Lars Göran Johansson, Seiichi Kawasaki, Fraser Mendel, Daniela Riccardi, Michael Ricks, Tom Behrens Sorensen, Michael Treschow and Jöerg Wuttke.

Johan Björkstén & Anders Hägglund
December, 2009

Contents

Preface

I wish I had written this book myself years ago. I have always felt I would have needed something like this when I first started pursuing my business career in China in the late 1980s.

Looking at the towering skyscrapers of Beijing and Shanghai, it is difficult to imagine that the Chinese economic miracle is only some three decades old. Back in the early days of Chinese business, there was little guidance to be had — my colleagues and I learned from our own mistakes, or if lucky, from the problems others faced, as we went along. Some 10 years ago, an initial trickle of business books rapidly grew into a flood. I have read many of the countless titles that have since appeared on the market. Few of them are excellent, and most tend to fall into two categories: academic treatises of the Chinese business environment, or entertaining, often literary, accounts of the exploits of individual businessmen as they navigate the exotic shoals of the Chinese market. Until now, I have hardly found a practical handbook written by active business people with on-the-ground management experience.

So why does this book fill a need? Why do we need a handbook for doing business in China? As a result of my work with the European Chamber of Commerce here, I have come to realize that the lessons that I and other early entrants learned are still relevant today. Although the Chinese market has matured rapidly as the result of growth and global integration, there are still plenty of pitfalls, and companies entering China in the early 21st century tend to make some of the very same mistakes that we all did in the 1980s and 1990s. Based on their own experience, and that of other seasoned "China hands", Johan Björkstén and Anders Hägglund provide hands-on, practical advice that can help managers avoid repeating the most common errors. Their reference checklists may be useful not only to new arrivals, but also to anyone managing a business here.

The authors acknowledge that "China is different"; this may sound like a platitude, but is still important to keep in mind. Even after 20 years doing business in China, the truisms like "China is different" are the insights that most of us "know", but hardly constantly practice. China is more like a large and diverse continent than a country; its business culture and history sometimes differently interprets business concepts and systems that seem superficially similar or even identical to Western ideas; and in many areas, China has unique traditions that influence every aspect of enterprise, from legal issues to the elusive but often mission-critical feel for "the way things are done around here".

[margin note: Perpetuate Stereo types?]

Yet, this assertion of "uniqueness", in my opinion, can also be a serious stumbling block for expatriate managers who fail to trust their own instincts and sometimes allow respect for "cultural differences" to overshadow common sense. It is therefore refreshing to see that, even as they highlight the differences, the authors avoid the mistake of overemphasizing cultural factors, of making China seem more "mysterious" than it actually is. Instead, they provide an unusually down-to-earth and operational perspective on the Chinese marketplace.

[margin note: Must learn norms]

[margin note: It should nt be]

China is rapidly developing into an economic and political world power, the largest economic comeback story the world has ever seen. I believe it is essential for economic success as well as for international relations that all of us, together with our Chinese partners, create a smooth, constructive, and successful local experience for international business here. This book is a valuable contribution to this ongoing effort.

[margin note: Multi-Polar environmen]

Jöerg Wuttke
Chairman, European Chamber of Commerce in China
Chief Representative, BASF China

Introduction

Why We Wrote This Book

This book is based on the experiences of two (very different) businessmen. In 1994, within a few months of each other, the two of us, Anders and Johan, arrived in China. Our missions, support and starting conditions could not have been more different: as the newly appointed 50-year-old boss of world-leading multinational toolmaker Sandvik, which ranked 650 on the Forbes 2000 list of global corporations, Anders was charged with building a profitable China operation for his company; Johan was a 30-year-old aspiring entrepreneur without any existing organization or support. Anders did not speak a word of Chinese; for him, China was *[handwritten: Went in blind]* yet another posting in a successful international career at a global corporation. Johan, on the other hand, was becoming fluent in the language and culture after having spent two years studying chemistry at "the Harvard of China", Peking University, and traveling *[handwritten: Immersion]* extensively around the country, meeting people in most of the major cities and even spending time among poor villagers in the rural hinterland.

China is a fascinating civilization, and a fascinating place to do business. For Anders, China was the chance of working with young, malleable recruits and shape an entrepreneurial subsidiary *[handwritten: Built]* almost from scratch. In this process, Anders could leverage the experience, systems, structures, and financial resources of a leading multinational, but he also quickly came to realize that most management tools had to be adapted to some extent to be suitable for the Chinese market environment. *[handwritten: Not all countries the same]*

For Johan, China was the opportunity of a lifetime — a dynamic market with huge potential that would allow a young

1

entrepreneur enormous freedom in building a company from scratch. Building a business did not come easily. Johan started, and shut down, a music record company and a trading company before making his third venture, Eastwei, a local success. Johan's companies have had to rely on money generated from the businesses themselves. There were no senior managers to rely on, no home organization to finance local expansion.

Over the last 10 years, we have been able to prove, each in his area, that it is possible to succeed as a foreign businessman in China. Anders built Sandvik's China business from a 30-person affair with turnover of less than 10 MUSD, to a thriving, profitable group of companies with more than 600 employees and revenues exceeding 200 MUSD. Johan's PR firm grew to a local leadership position with over 100 employees in four offices across China.

When, at the end of the 1990s, our paths crossed as board members in the Swedish Chamber of Commerce, we therefore quickly discovered that we already had many experiences in common. As our friendship developed, we often discussed Chinese business and management and gradually came to see that there were similarities in the way we ran our companies, similarities that were independent of different industries and company particulars.

1. Understanding and Managing China-Specific Issues

We found it particularly interesting that despite the differences between industries and detailed management styles of our companies — professional services on the one hand and the manufacturing and sales of industrial products on the other — and the fact that we did not share many superficial similarities in systems, processes, and structures, our basic recipes for success were remarkably similar. We discussed these lessons with managers from other successful companies in China and found that they often agreed with our viewpoints.

In this context, it is worth pointing out that in global business, we believe that there are more similarities than there are differences, but if we had chosen to focus on the similarities, we would perhaps have chosen a title like *How to be a successful manager (anywhere)*. In our experience, there are unique characteristics of the Chinese market that need to be taken into account, if one is to manage a China operation well. These are of two types: specific factors linked to local market conditions and Chinese business culture, and general aspects of working in an environment characterized by exceptionally fast growth and rapid change. The gaps in language and culture, as well as persistent myths surrounding the market, sometimes make it difficult to see these differences and similarities for what they are.

[margin note: No uniform approach]

[margin note: Important]

To succeed in China, we believe that managers need to

- Understand the fundamentals and characteristics of the China market; differences and similarities between China and other markets; differences within China; and the fact that China has changed and is changing fast.
- Adapt global business strategy to the Chinese reality while carefully maintaining integrity.
- Involve themselves directly in execution and control.
- Communicate effectively with head office to maintain understanding and support.

[margin note: Comms & adaptation]

Some or all of these statements will be familiar; a few may even feel hackneyed. But we will try to use this simple framework as a backdrop for providing concrete and specific advice which we hope will help managers interpret the local business environment and support day-to-day decision making.

[margin note: For a reason]

2. China Holds Lessons for a Globalized World

As we started writing the book, however, we came to another, even more interesting conclusion. We have come to believe that the

Chinese experience offers important general lessons for what it means to work in a globalized business environment.

[handwritten: Mix of free/closed]

Some areas in China are tightly regulated. But the majority of industries and segments of the Chinese economy are actually some of the most open, and therefore most competitive, markets in the world. Take, for example, household appliances. In developed countries, markets have been dominated by a few brands with strong, locally established businesses: Whirlpool and GE in America, Electrolux and Siemens in Europe, National and Hitachi in Japan, LG and Samsung in Korea. But in China, *all* of these companies are present — together with dozens of aggressive local competitors, formidable challengers by dint of aspiration, flexibility and locally entrenched markets as well as sheer hunger and determination to succeed at almost any cost. In banking, the major multinationals are slugging it out to get a head start while competing with burgeoning local giants. The car market typifies the experience of other industries: a prolonged period of heavy, loss-making investment followed by intense competition and then by oversupply as first Chrysler, VW, GM, Peugeot and Toyota, and finally almost everyone else, went head over heels to establish a presence and build market share under the intense scrutiny of hundreds of hungry, fast-learning local competitors, many of whom had international ambitions and some of whom had different ethical standards.

[handwritten: More compet. in local markets]

As markets around the world open up, these Chinese industries offer case studies that point the way to the future. We have come to think that China is a "time machine" that will allow industry leaders to better understand, and prepare for, the future of business in their home markets as they become increasingly exposed to competition from emerging countries. We also believe China can work as a greenhouse for training future corporate leaders in an increasingly competitive world — expatriate managers trained in the challenging Chinese environment as well as highly educated and hardworking Chinese employees being trained for positions abroad.

[handwritten: Template]

We believe China has profound implications for business in the 21st century — not only because of the direct effects the country is having on companies around the world, but also because China itself offers a case study in globalization and thus of a future, more competitive, business environment. We hope that you will agree with our conclusions — and that you will enjoy sharing some of the fun we have had, and the challenges that we have weathered, in this fascinating country.

Chapter 1

Chinese Business Climate

1.1. Land of Golden Opportunity or Corporate Quagmire?

Are foreign companies successful in China? Over the two decades or so that foreign businesses have again been involved in the Chinese market in a major way, opinions have differed. There is the pessimistic camp, according to which foreigners have forever chased the potential of China without ever realizing any profits. In his book, *The China Dream*, Joe Studwell traces these aspirations over hundreds of years, starting with the 17th century efforts of Jesuit monks such as Matteo Ricci to convert "a single market of 150 million souls" to Christianity, and continuing with the railway investment bonanza of the late 19th century and Carl Crow's 1937 classic *Four hundred million customers*, to finally provide a series of case studies of failed investments in the 1990s and early 2000s. According to Studwell, the China investment frenzy is based on hype based on a misunderstanding of the fundamentals underpinning the Chinese economic reality, as well as underestimation of the difficulties and obstacles involved in doing business in the country.

Doing business in China is not as easy as the headquarters of multinational corporations think. The potential is there, but business cannot live off potential alone. As the world's largest recipient of foreign direct investment (FDI), China has certainly been host to an increasing number of multinational companies who have, in some cases, floundered and lost money for years, and in other cases simply given up on the market after losses accumulated to unacceptable levels.

7

There is, however, also a more optimistic point of view. If by "success" we mean "profitable growth", that is, "showing long-term, steady growth while maintaining a profit level acceptable to the owners", most companies actually seem to be doing reasonably well in China; some have even been spectacularly successful. Well-known multinational corporations such as ABB, BASF, Coca-Cola, GE, IKEA, Nestle, P&G, Siemens, SONY, and Volkswagen can, to date, all be counted as resounding success stories in China. They have been accompanied by tens of thousands of lesser-known enterprises who are showing every sign of having made the right investment decisions. Surveys on the local business climate carried out by the Chambers of Commerce of various countries also seem to indicate that member companies tend to show higher and higher profits as they become more familiar with the local market.

1.2. From Manufacturing Base to Competitive Market

It is important to differentiate between the — usually successful and profitable — companies who use China as a manufacturing base, and the companies who have tried to break into the local marketplace by selling their goods or services there. Local manufacturing seems to be relatively straightforward; local marketing and distribution have been the toughest nuts to crack. But as the market grows, matures and becomes more relatively important on a global scale, and as Chinese companies start entering the world markets, more and more multinationals need to do exactly that: compete with these new entrants on their home turf. This is the macroscopic situation we deal within this book.

1.3. More Demanding Head Offices

It is true that some companies have suffered large losses on the local Chinese market. But as international head offices have become more knowledgeable about China, they have also become more demanding of their local organizations. A few years ago, multinationals would accept loss-making subsidiaries because it was seen as "investing in the market". Today, most companies demand profitability of their China operations and tend to regard China as "just another market".

1.4. A Welcoming Business Climate...

Multinational companies are, overall, also manifestly welcome in China. In neighboring Korea and Japan, foreign companies have been met with more ambiguous feelings. Overall, the Chinese acceptance of foreigners and things foreign has been high, almost to the point of being overbearingly welcoming from time to time. When one of us mentioned the fact that "I feel very welcome in China" to a Chinese colleague, her reply was "that is only natural; we learn in school to like foreigners". Multinational companies have in many cases received substantially preferential treatment compared to Chinese private and even state-owned enterprises, to the extent that Chinese enterprises started investing in holding companies abroad in order to come back as "foreigners" to invest in China, taking advantage of the tax breaks, importation policies and VAT refunds that "real" foreign companies enjoy. These benefits have been particularly pronounced in the so-called special economic zones. Here, foreign companies usually get easy access to policy makers who can help solve administrative problems. The zones are established as a way to provide easy access to resources, workers, and policies.

1.5. ...Or the Heavy Hand of the State?

The more pessimistic crowd would regard these successes as isolated areas in a difficult macro environment of low development, ambiguous laws, arbitrary restrictions, and control. In China, they would emphasize, you will often compete against government agencies that belong to the state bureaucracy issuing regulations for your industry. The field is hopelessly slanted in favor of Chinese state-owned enterprises and "market" conditions are determined by ham-handed bureaucrats in love with grandiose policies bordering on the megalomaniac.

In his book, *One Billion Customers*, Jim McGregor describes his own fight, as head of Dow Jones's business operations in China, with the vested interests of the Xinhua news agency. By bureaucratic fiat, Xinhua simply issued regulations that outlawed its international competitors from the Chinese market. The same thing has happened in other industries; a hugely successful foreign entrepreneur in language education one day received a letter signed by the main Chinese language universities stating that the Ministry of Education had "decided to shut him down for unfair competition" and asking him to abide by this decision. In the end, however, both McGregor and our entrepreneur friend succeeded in deflecting such attacks and their businesses continued to thrive in China.

1.6. The Wild East

We once heard Frédéric Cho, an "old China hand" with some 20 years of experience from the Chinese market working for major financial institutions like Banque Indosuez, talk to a delegation of visiting European parliamentarians. "Which are the main obstacles to success on the Chinese market?" they asked. "How can we ensure that companies become profitable in China?" As Frédéric rattled off one suggestion after the other, the politicians looked more and more confused. "Excuse me", one of them interrupted, "but it sounds like you are blaming the companies themselves, rather than Chinese policy, for most failures in China". "That is correct", replied Frédéric. "Most companies fail in China through their own incompetence. When a company has problems, it is perfectly natural for the managers responsible to blame China for their own failures. But when you look at the specifics of each case, you quickly see that management failed to understand the market, chose the wrong partners or simply underestimated the challenges of doing business in China, all of which could have been avoided had the company done its homework correctly".

Jöerg Wuttke, Chief Representative for German chemicals giant BASF and himself an old China hand with long local experience, notes that "everybody blames China, but when you analyze failed ventures, you usually find that the mistakes were their own. The perception is so different from the mature markets like the US, where European companies usually admit that the errors are of our own making". The myth of the "difficult Chinese market" is also influenced by media reports and books claiming that many, even most, multinationals are losing money in the country. Wuttke continues: "People complain about unfair competition. But most multinationals do make money. China is a profitable place to do business — with 10% market growth, it is actually pretty hard to fail here".

Depending on one's mindset and experience, it is possible to take either a very optimistic or a pessimistic view of the Chinese market. We have known and talked with international business people of each persuasion. The general consensus tends to be that, sure, there may be great opportunities, but there are also innumerable pitfalls for the unwary.

This is why we often compare China, "The Wild East", to the Wild West of Hollywood renown: the opportunities are endless on this new frontier, but the businessman without his wits about him may end up losing everything. By this we do not mean to say that Chinese businesspeople are less trustworthy or more corrupt than businessmen elsewhere or that the Chinese business environment is hopelessly stacked against the foreigner — just that China is such a large, complex, and dynamic marketplace that you need to be even more vigilant and astute than on more mature markets. To do business, you will still need to develop fruitful relationships with partners and employees whom you are prepared to trust.

1.7. What You as a Manager can Influence

Whether or not China is "difficult" is beside the focus of this book. Complaining about "unfair competition" is, in our opinion, simply irrelevant for the individual manager; it is difficult for the individual to do anything about. A businessman has to do his best to succeed by adapting to the situation he is facing — or opt out of the market, as the case may be.

In China, we can often influence our own situation to an unusually high degree. We are facing a blank slate without legacies. It is not unusual for foreign entrants to be able to "define the market", just as is the case for new industries in the West. Just as dotcoms such as Amazon defined the online retail market, and a brand like Listerine once created, or at least made relevant, the concept of chronic halitosis, so Häagen-Dasz ice cream has defined its very own premium segment in China. Häagen-Dasz is sold at higher prices in China than in the US and Europe, despite the much lower average income levels in China. Häagen-Dasz ice cream parlors have become the venue of choice for middle-class Chinese to hold a romantic rendezvous.

Ogilvy and Mather, a respected advertising agency with a me-too offering in PR and integrated marketing services in other countries, has made itself into the market leader in most of its areas of activity in China. The secret? By being an early mover, and taking a long-term approach to building its organization, the firm has successfully leveraged its advertising brand into other areas of activity and gained respectability in a wide range of businesses.

Which are the factors you can influence, and which ones must you learn to live with? What can you learn from the mistakes and triumphs of those who have gone before you? How much can and should you adapt to local conditions? How much can you compromise your business idea and corporate core values in order to adjust to China? If it is possible at least for *some* companies in a wide range of businesses to "succeed" in China, can we then try to find some of the factors that have made them successful? And what can we learn from their less fortunate peers, who in China found only failed ambitions and missed opportunities?

Some of the factors where success is directly dependent on one's own actions, or which one can at least prepare for in an adequate way, are:

- Understanding of the market: culture, market research, choice of partners, due diligence, analysis of market barriers.
- Legal structure and geographic localization of business.
- Quality and motivation of management and of employees.
- Execution and follow-up.
- Realistic expectations and a sustainable mandate from head office.
- Consistency and endurance of policies.
- Marketing and brand building.

Of course, external factors will also influence success. There are political, social, and macroeconomic questions such as investment policies, benefits, and legal investment framework to consider. There are also internal corporate questions such as product offerings, management issues and China's overall role in global production strategies. We will focus on those issues that are in the direct sphere of influence of a local manager.

Chapter 2

Differences and Similarities

"I have been to countries where they drive on the right hand of the road and I have been to countries where they drive on the left — but this is the first time I've ever experienced a place where people drive on both sides", a business acquaintance visiting Shanghai in the 1990s once quipped to Johan. Although the situation on the streets of the largest Chinese cities is more orderly these days, we would still suggest that riding with a local cabbie is the ideal crash course in Chinese business for the newly arrived foreign executive. Your taxi driver's freethinking interpretation of traffic regulations closely mimics the way Chinese businesspeople have learned to maneuver a heavily regulated, contradictory and chaotic local business environment.

After half an hour on the road, you will have come to fully appreciate the commonly heard saying among expatriate businessmen: "In China, everything is difficult but nothing is impossible".

2.1. Sources of Some Differences from Other Markets

China will likely be different from other countries where an international manager has worked. Some of the characteristics that determine these differences are:

- *Size*: China is a very large country; cultural and economic differences between regions are often wide. In addition, lack of logistics solutions and internal trade barriers make some markets difficult to access.
- *Market development*: China is not yet a fully developed market economy and systems and institutions can be lacking or immature. Aspects of the planned economy continue to influence some industries.
- *Cultural factors*: Chinese people relate to each other, and to the environment, in ways that are subtly different from Westerners. Only by understanding such differences can you successfully negotiate with Chinese business partners and manage local coworkers. China also has a long tradition of education and self-betterment; this influences how Chinese colleagues view employment opportunities and long-term careers.
- *Low trust*: During the planned economy era, when there was not a lot of competition in the market, both consumers and corporate customers could do little if they were cheated and left with the short end of the stick. There is still a "trust deficit", where customers are afraid of being cheated. This has sometimes worked to the advantage of multinational companies, which were often automatically held to higher standards than local companies. This situation is changing, as more and more Chinese companies have grown large and mature enough to care about their reputation in the market. Even so, building trust is important in China: Besides being as wary as a local business person on your own part,

you also need to build a strong brand that communicates trust-worthiness. And it is not only customers who are suspicious — building trust with employees takes time as well.

All of these factors, taken together, mean that things do not always happen as quickly and easily as one would hope. Endurance, patience, and carefully considered long-term objectives are key.

2.2. Some "China" Factors with Global Relevance

There are also aspects of the Chinese market that can be said to be equally valid in other countries or business segments. In our opin-ion, China has much in common with other markets, and Chinese employees are often motivated by the same factors as their col-leagues in the US or Europe are.

Some especially salient "China factors" that we believe will become more relevant world-wide as a result of globalization are:

- *Rapid change*: During the last decades, China has embarked on a breakneck journey to break out of poverty and backwardness. But the most striking changes are not the improvements in material conditions and all the new skyscrapers breaking up the skylines of Chinese cities; the real revolution is happening in the social and psychological environment. Values, attitudes, ways of life are in flux. This happens everywhere as societies adapt to globalization with the resulting increase in competi-tion, complexity and international contacts. But in China, this global phenomenon combines with the legacies of a laissez-faire business culture and lack of social safety nets, with the result that Chinese employees pay attention to job security and often prefer working for a stable, reputable company rather than a small startup.
- *Most businesses are relatively new*: Business in China is usually about rapidly building and growing to keep up with the mar-ket, rather than streamlining and consolidating an existing organization. In understanding China, we can learn a lot from

the global experiences of new industries such as IT and the dotcom boom.

- *Growth will be high-speed*: Most industries are developing very rapidly in China. This means that, for most companies, taking and consolidating market share should be one of the main business objectives even in bulk industries such as energy and commodities. When the markets mature, market positions will become less volatile and companies who have taken the lion's share in their industry can expect to reap handsome rewards.

- *The market is hyper-competitive*: Although some industries in China are protected or heavily regulated, the majority are among the most open in the world. Because of the huge potential, most of your international competitors will be present and fighting for long-term market share with a horde of local companies joining the fray using cut-throat prices to compete. This trend is already becoming apparent globally, resulting in consumer prices being pushed down and cozy market positions being eroded in a matter of months.

For those managers who ran companies during the headiest days of the dotcom era, none of this is new — it is just that China has been living through what is already above 30 years of such explosive growth and competition for market share and talent. The management lessons from the IT sector in Europe and the US of the late 20th century are often applicable to the Chinese reality. This also means that local employees and managers have little or no experience of difficult times or even normal business cycles.

This challenging business climate also tends to accentuate management issues that are of a more general nature. When you find yourself managing an immature workforce in a rapidly changing environment, mistakes are easier to make and tend to have graver consequences than in a more developed market. China can thus in some cases also serve to highlight more generally applicable truths about good management. As we mention in the foreword, we believe that China offers "a glimpse of things to come" in a globalized world.

2.3. Common Myths about China

As we have seen, it is true that China is in some ways "different"; flexibility and adaptability to local conditions are important. But there are also many who would portray the Chinese market as even more difficult and mysterious than it really is. There are several ways that this happens:

- *Cultural differences are exaggerated*: In most cases, "cultural" differences are actually rational reactions to objective criteria such as local conditions, economy, and recent history. By understanding the context of local actors, we can easily understand the rationale behind their behavior.
- *Individual differences are misinterpreted as generalities*: We have seen instances where international colleagues have drawn wide-ranging conclusions based on impressions or information from one or two Chinese individuals.
- *Cultural differences are used deliberately*: Local colleagues often attempt to argue their case by claiming that "this is the way things are done in China". Such argumentation can lead to a slippery slope when you deal with sensitive issues such as corruption. Some consultants also seem to deliberately mystify China, perhaps in order to justify their own existence.
- *Myths become accepted truths*: In the 1970s, it was an accepted "truth" that the authorities installed listening devices to eavesdrop on all foreigners in China; in modern management circles, people often claim that Chinese employees are somehow less loyal or more prone to jump ship than their counterparts in other parts of the world.

2.4. A Diverse and Heterogeneous Market

Perhaps the most important myth is the recurring reference to the concept of "the Chinese". Business authors sometimes treat China as if it were one monolithic, coordinated bureaucratic machine dealing with "the foreigners" so as to maximize benefits for itself. In the 1970s, perhaps even the 1980s and early 1990s, it may still have been relevant to see Chinese business negotiation efforts as coordinated on a national level. At that time, foreign firms had to negotiate with central "buying organizations" which acted on behalf of local customers. At the dreaded Erligou "negotiation building" close to the Diaoyutai State Guesthouse in Western Beijing, businessmen would be given time slots for discussions and thereafter subjected to a harrowing wait outside the venue, trying to interpret the expressions on the faces of competitors who had gone before them in the negotiation cycle as these came out of their sessions with the Chinese hosts.

Today, buying decisions are made by the corporations themselves, be they private or state-owned. Central, government-led negotiations are the norm only for very large infrastructure projects or areas perceived of critical importance to Chinese development. Even the best business guides available, such as Lucian W. Pye's *Chinese Negotiating Style*, must therefore be read with the modern market in mind when they refer to cases such as the "major American firm that [...] had waited three years after making its formal presentations and signing letters of intent for *the Chinese* to say they are ready to engage in the final, substantive negotiations" (our italics). Such cases are the exception, not the rule, today — although they may still apply to business dealings with state monopolies or government administrations.

China is a complex, dynamic market economy, albeit with strong remnants of the old state economy still in place. There is usually a lot of choice in just which "Chinese" to deal with these days. The typical modern executive should simply walk away from its glacial negotiation counterpart in Pye's example and seek a better partner with which to develop his business. It is also important to recognize that the Chinese government, in whatever incarnation you interact with it, is dealing with the same challenges — immaturities, rapid growth, and so on — that you are. By recognizing that you share some of the challenges, you may find it easier to work in synergy with your Chinese government partners.

2.5. Do You Really Need to be in China?

Another common misconception is the oft-repeated statement that "our company must have a presence in China". The reasons for this perception may be an overestimation of the market potential, herd mentality ("all our competitors are there") or failure to appreciate the difficulties of establishing a sustainable business in China. Building an international presence is always fraught with difficulties. To Europeans, the US market is a notoriously expensive and difficult nut to crack. But China combines the American market problem of size and complexity with underdeveloped institutions, cultural differences, and rapid change. The first question that any businessman should ask himself must therefore be: "Why do we really need to be in China?"

2.6. Common Sense Solutions

The size and dynamism of China can be intoxicating. We have seen intelligent, experienced, and mature Western businesspeople make some pretty outrageous mistakes, mistakes that they would never have committed back home. On the one hand, there is a widespread superiority complex, where the Western party sees himself as somehow more advanced than the Chinese party. On the other hand, Westerners sometimes come to China with an inherent sense of being "supplicants asking for Chinese beneficence". It seems to us that Western businessmen often commit errors because they are either too arrogant, or too eager to adapt themselves to what somebody has told them is customary (or taboo) in China, or claimed is "just how things are done here".

This overcompensation for perceived "cultural differences" is so prevalent that we will be returning to it regularly throughout the book. Most of the challenges to understanding we have listed above stem from factual differences in market development and macro environment rather than some notion of "cultural" differences. By relying on a correct analysis of objective market conditions, and by combining this understanding with your own business experience and a good portion of common sense, it is not hard to avoid the worst mistakes. The basic business advice must therefore be to simply trust your instincts!

On the other hand, there are legal and administrative areas where differences in locally established practice compared to Western countries are so large that you may actually find them difficult to explain to your home office. One such area is the use of chops or personal seals instead of signatures — in China, such stamps often take the place of powers of attorney or affidavits, which means that corporate and personal chops must be managed in a deliberate and controlled fashion. But practical differences of this kind can usually be clearly explained and dealt with in a defined way — there is nothing mysterious about them.

So are there really no cultural differences at all between Chinese and Westerners? Of course there are. And we need to understand and work with these cultural issues in order to feel more comfortable doing business in China. But ostensible "cultural differences" should never be a reason to throw common sense overboard. As Fraser Mendel, an American lawyer with years of experience from on-the-ground legal work in China, advises his clients: "If someone in China says something that wouldn't feel right back home in Chicago, then it's probably not going to fly in China either".

The way to success, then, is to base decisions on your own experience and gut feeling, while at the same time trying your best to understand Chinese business culture. Let us begin by analyzing some of the cultural differences that do exist, and look at how we can work with or around them.

Chapter 3

Key Concepts of Chinese Business Culture

In order to start sorting out the unique cultural factors from more generally applicable truths, let us first look at two oft-mentioned cultural phenomena which influence all aspects of doing business in China: "face" and "guanxi".

3.1. Face — Making Other People Look Good

Face is a pervasive concept both in business settings and in Chinese family and personal life. "Giving face" means showing that you care for another person: by listening intently and responding in an appropriate and constructive way, by providing help when asked for a favor, and by actively putting the other party in a good light in front of other people, especially superiors and other influential persons. Giving face is different from just "being a nice guy" or "helping out" — the face aspect emphasizes the social context, the fact that the other party is made to look good in front of others.

The opposite of giving face, causing someone to "lose face" through demonstrating lack of respect, referring to mistakes or criticizing in public, or a refusal to come forth with, at least moral support, is frowned upon.

3.2. Giving, and Saving, Face

A key cultural competency for any manager in China is managing face for her employees. You must go to great lengths to avoid putting your colleagues in positions where they perceive themselves as having lost face. The emphasis here is on "perceive" — loss of face is a subjective matter. Typical situations that can cause a perceived loss of face are:

- Being upbraided or criticized in front of others.
- Promotion of a colleague.
- A new job role.
- Being asked to report to someone more junior, even on a short-term project.

Any manager will of course from time to time need to deliver constructive criticism, promote people, or assemble cross-functional teams where the most senior manager may not be the most qualified leader. How can we deal with such issues without causing our colleagues to lose face? Timing, context, and communication matter.

- *Avoid criticism in front of others*: If you need to discuss performance on a particular issue, do it behind closed doors. This does not mean you have to put on kid gloves. It is OK to be quite straightforward, just avoid public embarrassment.
- *Take into consideration the face issues of all colleagues concerned when you promote a coworker or assemble a team*: Anders once promoted a colleague to a managerial position, only to have several colleagues who had not been promoted hand in their resignation letters. It turned out that this was not a simple case of these colleagues feeling "passed over" or a lack of future opportunity, but a feeling that they would lose face vis-à-vis other colleagues because of a perceived difference in seniority to the promoted manager. The problem was solved by providing new titles for all parties concerned. Oftentimes, you can find a way of preparing for and presenting a promotion to avoid others being embarrassed. Transparency helps here, too — paradoxically, it seems that people feel less loss of face if the objective reasons

for the promotion of a colleague are made clear. Being upfront about the rationale for team composition avoids misinterpretations that could otherwise have lead to a perceived loss of face.

- *Encourage feedback*: If your Chinese colleagues are given the opportunity to provide regular input into your decisions, you lower the risk of blindsiding coworkers in a way that could cause them to lose face.
- *Use face to your advantage*: Sometimes, such as in a conflict or a negotiation context, the Westerner's lack of consideration for his or her own face can provide a competitive advantage — it is easy to simply accept responsibility for a problem and move on, something that may be more difficult for a Chinese colleague to do.

3.3. Guanxi — Business Relationships

The first thing most foreign businessmen will hear about doing business in China is the importance of "guanxi" (pronounced *gwan-shee*, with the stress on the first syllable), literally "relationships". Chinese people are generally more dependent on the people around them than are Westerners. This does not necessarily mean that Chinese people are not individualists — just that they are more attuned to the needs and sentiments of other people. Chinese people will also generally be more used to asking for and providing support than most Westerners.

Guanxi is without doubt one of the most important concepts to master for anyone wanting to do business with China — and at the same time one of the most misunderstood and over-mystified. It is also often portrayed as a "negative" aspect of China, linked to corrupt and unethical practices. Let us try to define the term a bit more carefully, and then have a look at how to practically go about building guanxi.

Guanxi is often translated as "contacts" or "relations", but these English terms tend to carry negative connotations of impenetrable "old boys" networks, whereas the Chinese term is usually used in a positive sense. Guanxi is a complex term, which, depending on context, can have several connotations:

- A relationship that implies mutual benefit: "I have excellent guanxi with the local water bureau — I helped them apply for their visas to Europe last year, and they have solved the water problems for our factory on several occasions".
- A statement of confidence that the person will help a particular person if asked to do so: "Our local GM has excellent guanxi with the Mayor, so if we have problems, we can always ask him for support".
- A way of giving face and establishing a relationship: "I have excellent guanxi with them; I invited their chairman to hold a speech at the Chamber of Commerce last year".
- A networked view of the world, a problem-solving approach that uses contact networks to quickly find information or solve problems: "I called some guanxi in the industry, and it seems that what we are dealing with is actually a rather common problem. They suggest we solve it by...".

A recent university essay on guanxi by Nils Hedberg defined the concept as "a Chinese system of favors emphasizing trust, often founded on... common experiences". Guanxi-relationships are based on a mutual, often, but not always, warm and personal reciprocity between individuals. This in turn is related to how Chinese people traditionally care for family, relatives, and friends.

Social anthropologists talk about the "large" circle (society) and the "small" circle (family and friends); Western cultures tend to give priority to the large circle and Chinese prioritize the small circle. If you have ever had the fortune to have a Chinese person as a host, you will be familiar with the lengths a Chinese person will go to in order to accommodate and care for guests and friends. This mindset has probably been further reinforced by the turbulent centuries where society often lacked the power to protect the individual — or was even the source of oppression. The personal network, the "guanxi wang", was the only social safety net one could trust. If you want to develop a business relationship with a Chinese company, you need to demonstrate respect for ("give face to") the people in the relationship.

3.3.1. *Avoid trusting empty claims to guanxi*

For several years, a Fortune-500 company negotiated without success to build a major joint-venture production base in China. Promised by "the Chinese" that the startup was just a matter of "a few more signatures" the company set up a local organization of some 50 people to plan and prepare for production. The company took much of its advice from a well-paid consultant, an overseas Chinese in his late 30s, who claimed high-level contacts in the Chinese government. According to the people we talked to at the company in question, he repeatedly "proved" these relations by arranging meetings for the company's visiting CEO with leading Chinese government figures.

Given the liberal Chinese investment policies, one might wonder why it took several years for the company to get its (much downsized) factory, given the consultant's claim to such excellent guanxi in the Chinese government — and who, exactly, were "the Chinese authorities" purportedly holding up the decision? As for the consultant's ability to arrange top-level meetings, we would like to claim that if you gave one of our capable secretaries (who, as far as we know, do not have any special relations in the higher circles of the Chinese government) the CEO of a Fortune-500 company as "door opener" she would be able to set up meetings with some pretty senior people too. Chinese politicians focus on investments and the economy, and regularly meet with high-ranking international business people.

The moral of the story: being led to believe that guanxi is something "different" or "mysterious" can be costly. Business is business; the way to build guanxi is to show that you care, that you are trustworthy, and that you are in the relationship for the long term.

3.3.2. *Guanxi is less important than before*

In a planned economy, where companies had few business incentives, good guanxi was often the only way of ensuring access to products and services. Developing relationships with influential people were also the way to get ahead in a heavily politicized system. Even in the 1980s, little could be accomplished in China without recourse to networks of personal contacts. The same situation still prevails today in heavily regulated industries or when your main customers are state-owned companies or government institutions.

Today, however, we believe that the perceived importance of guanxi is the single most exaggerated myth of doing business in China.

It is true that the word guanxi is difficult to translate with a single term. Guanxi can refer to a particular relationship, or to the set of relationships a particular person has at her disposal; her network or how "connected" she is. Guanxi can also denote the degree of trust in a relationship or how professionally or privately useful the relationship can be.

It is also true that guanxi still plays a huge role in China. The country has lived through a difficult 20th century. Wars, disasters, and political campaigns ravaged the country. The absence of a strong state taught people that they must mainly rely on themselves, or a closely knit network of friends and acquaintances, to survive.

This means that corruption, for example, can be "guanxi-driven". If you encounter corruption it will not be of the flagrant kind that requires you to pay a "tip" in order to receive some officially free government service. Corruption in China, even when it involves money, is usually between people who know and trust each other. It also means that some government functions, such as licensing of certain kinds of business, will be susceptible to influence by personal relationships. This is especially the case in gray areas where the legal system or government policy is unclear.

In situations of scarcity, such as the recurring electricity brownouts that plague some industries, good guanxi is probably still the best way of minimizing your company's exposure.

But in summary we believe the guanxi concept is overrated, for two main reasons:

- Because guanxi is a straightforward and operational business concept rather than a "smoke-filled room". There is nothing mysteriously "Chinese" about it.
- Because trusting the guanxi claims of local employees and consultants can cost companies dearly.

3.3.3. *Guanxi — Networking the Chinese way*

Guanxi is built through commitment and thoughtfulness. It is both the foundation of business relationships, and the result of them. Trust is a key component of guanxi, and establishing trust takes time. But once the guanxi is created, the benefits are great. Watching a Chinese networker in action is a real joy; confronted with any problem (Where to buy a good computer? Who can best fix the carburetor of my imported Porsche? Where to find a GM for my Guangzhou office? How to apply for a visa to Germany?), he instinctively turns to his contacts — who in turn call their contacts, who call theirs, until a solution is sent back down the network. It is also these contacts of contacts that offer a room to stay, when a Chinese person pays a tourist visit to London for a few days.

Brokers in information, the Chinese guanxi artists are constantly on their cell phones, sometimes to the chagrin of Western business colleagues who are used to a different brand of phone etiquette. Guanxi grows through contact and mutual support — and asking for a favor can sometimes create as much guanxi as giving one — but also through ongoing contacts; even when there is no immediate need for interaction, the network is still kept alive through a few extra phone calls, New Year cards, and mobile phone text messages — billions are sent for Chinese New Year annually. And of course one takes the opportunity to carry a package on behalf of guanxi A to A's grandmother in Shanghai, when one has reason to travel there, and a few little gifts to guanxi B from one's own business trip to the USA, as a signal that B has not been forgotten.

In fact, guanxi has less to do with a members-only social club, and more with what Western management consultants call "networking", albeit at an even deeper and more personal level — a way to get more things done, in a faster and simpler way, by fully utilizing the resources in one's circle of contacts. Simply put, Chinese people prefer doing business with people they know. This, of course, is true to some extent in other cultures as well.

Here are five laws about guanxi:

- Every person has a guanxi network.
- Guanxi is not (necessarily) something one is born with.
- Guanxi can be built and maintained in a systematic fashion.
- Guanxi has to be built with patience and over time.
- Guanxi should be built in advance, before you need them.

Note that these "rules" are operative, not just a general statement of "how important guanxi are". The five rules actually tell us that it is possible to write a business plan for developing one's guanxi in China. If you are familiar with the concepts of Relationship Marketing theory, you will feel right at home: it is all about creating and actively maintaining relationships with people and groups who impact your business. In China, such relationships are often long term; you become "old friends", as the Chinese put it, referring to a lifelong trusting and often mutually beneficial relationship.

3.3.4. *Guanxi is a straightforward business concept*

To see how guanxi functions operationally, let us look at the concept from a business perspective, based on our various translations above. If by "guanxi" we mean corrupt practices based on long-standing or inherited relationships that facilitate bending or working around official rules, this is rapidly losing in importance as the legal framework and day-to-day interpretation of rules in the Chinese market economy develops. There may still be "crony capitalists", the sons and daughters of well positioned and powerful individuals. But benefits from this kind of guanxi are seldom available to foreign companies in China.

If, on the other hand, we define guanxi as a general "lubricant" of business transactions, an age-old system by which Chinese people relate to each other, then there is nothing mysterious about the concept; indeed, this aspect of business is prevalent anywhere in the world and is the subject of international books on so-called "relationship marketing" theory. Visit any US ivy-league school or country golf club and you will see guanxi, western-style, in action in the form of fraternities, Masonic societies, and the friendship bonds that grow out of a shared college experience. Chinese people are, in modern business parlance, superb networkers (as we have seen, guanxi can be translated as either "relationships" or "networks").

In China, this understanding of guanxi is closely tied to the way that people interact on a daily level; most major business transactions will be based on a sense of mutual trust that can only be developed over a certain, albeit in no way unlimited, period of time. The idea can be summarized succinctly: Chinese prefer doing business with people they know.

We believe that the guanxi concept is relevant to foreign business people in China, but the distinction above is important, because it transforms an obscure cultural phenomenon into an operational part of personal as well as corporate business strategy.

3.3.5. *You must be in charge of your own guanxi*

Guanxi can be built and transferred from person to person. People have different talent for creating guanxi, but we all have a circle of friends and relatives that we have established over the years. Instead of trusting self-proclaimed insiders or consultants, you must *create* the guanxi you need in China. Maybe you will need a professional door opener from time to time, but in order for the relation to be useful and effective, you yourself, or at least your company, must "own" the contact. Doing this requires conscious effort, time, and a bit of discipline.

As a foreigner, you are actually sometimes at an advantage in creating guanxi. Overall, China is open, curious, and interested in things foreign. Chinese officials often actively desire contacts with foreign business people and politicians. You can exploit this by systematically getting to know, and giving face to, the people who will influence your Chinese business.

You also need to encourage and document the existing networks of your Chinese colleagues. Chinese people may be excellent at relationship building, but they tend to see these relationship as something purely individual; they lack systematic methods for recording and building networks in an organizational context. Databases and technologies for Customer Relations Management (CRM), are especially important in China. You should demand of your sales team that they document customer contacts — one of our American clients pay bonuses to salespeople only after they have updated the company customer database. Similarly, you should require that senior managers record their government contacts, that the PR manager has a database of journalists, and so on. In this way, you ensure that these networks become embedded as part of your company's intellectual property in China, and do not walk out the door when individual employees do.

Guanxi is not limited to the arena of business. In China, you will need to develop "personal" guanxi with your local tax authority and other organizations. The mutual trust that is fostered as part of guanxi building will facilitate any dealings you have with outside stakeholders. This does not mean you will have to resort to corrupt practices in China. It simply means that fostering good working relationships will make virtually every business dealing easier. Some would actually go so far as to say that managers need to develop good guanxi with their local employees. Perhaps this form of "guanxi" would be more accurately called a "focus on soft skills" — in other words, the ability to interrelate with coworkers on a social and emotional level. A 2006 study by Dr Nandani Lynton and Kirsten Høgh Thøgersen, published in *Organizational Dynamics*, explains that Chinese business managers showed much stronger competencies in these so-called "soft skills" than their Western peers: "Although feelings are rarely expressed in words, the Chinese expect business to be personal".

3.3.6. *Guanxi checklist*

Some of the operational conclusions that follow from the discussion above can be summarized as:

- *Guanxi is not primarily something you are born with*. Guanxi is an acquired way of relating to people by exchanging favors and giving face — in the business setting, showing that you respect and care about the other person as a human being, not just as a means to an end. Guanxi is not some mysterious, abstract phenomenon. Guanxi is built over time with the right people.
- *You need to develop your own guanxi*. Some companies try to take a shortcut to high-level connections by hiring a so-called "princeling", the son or daughter of a high-ranking government official. This can create internal problems, since the princeling may be difficult to manage and, because of his or her exalted position, does not necessarily need to be a very good or caring manager. It is usually a better idea to keep such persons at arm's length by using them as well-paid consultants. But even so, trusting consultants with your guanxi network is not a good idea. They can play an important role as door openers, but sooner or later you will have to "own" your own network of key relationships in order to ensure business security and success.
- *Guanxi must be created before you need it*. Chinese society is more relationship oriented than Western societies, so paying attention to the person behind the professional interaction becomes more important. Building trust is a process, not an action,

which means that it takes time. Whether in the more traditional sense of guanxi as a form of high-level access and facilitation, or in the wider sense of "soft skills", when the time comes to utilize your relationships, it is too late to start building them.

- *Guanxi need to be managed in a structured way*. This applies at the personal as well as corporate level. In China, spending time with stakeholders is part of your job. It is also imperative that you keep track of your relationships and that you give them face and show that you care about them. The little things, such as sending New Year's cards, count. On the company level, a good database can ensure that relationships are handed over in an effective way from one generation of management to the next. A change of GM or Marketing Manager should not have to mean that the company loses the previous manager's guanxi network.

These conclusions are equally relevant in a globalized marketplace. As competition increases, more and more companies offer products and services of a similar kind, at a similar price. The "differentiating factors" for business success then become perceptions, as embodied in the brand, and personal or institutionalized relationships. This is especially evident in business-to-business marketing, and has, together with new information technologies for consumer relationship building formed the impetus for "relationship marketing" theory.

3.4. Government Relations

3.4.1. *How important are government relations?*

One of the most prevalent myths about doing business in China is the importance of "government relations". One often hears businesspeople make sweeping comments on the crucial importance of government guanxi, or having a Chinese partner who "knows the system".

Sometimes, it appears to us that government relations are deemed important mainly as a perceived status symbol. Foreign managers seem to love having meetings with Chinese leaders for the prestige it brings to their own persons. Typically, managers from headquarters request meetings with government officials, and the local manager, eager to show that he or she has the right local connections, scrambles to make the appropriate arrangements. Having spent hours on the phone with recalcitrant junior officials (and more often than not anywhere from ten to two hundred thousand RMB on "consultants" who offer meetings with officials for a fee), the local manager succeeds in securing a 15-minute audience with a minister or mayor.

Such meetings tend to be ritualized. The foreign managers sit, in order of seniority, on one side of a u-shaped formation of chairs, with the Chinese officials on the other side. Senior managers and ranking cadres are placed in the middle, junior managers and minor officials at both ends of the u. The top manager and official exchange small talk over jasmine tea, express their admiration for the achievements of each others' countries and make vacuous commitments to contribute to continued fruitful relations. At the end, they exchange presents. The Chinese gift, usually a tacky specimen of local handicraft, will subsequently be prominently displayed in the visiting manager's office as a favorite focus of stories for visitors. "It was a gift from the Mayor of Shanghai", said one of our business acquaintances, proudly displaying the tasteless painting on his back wall and the photo of him shaking hands with the local bigwig. "Shanghai has more people than Sweden", he beamed, "so meeting this guy is like having a chat with the Prime Minister of a country".

But what exactly is the real value of such a meeting? The ceremonial format usually gives little or no room for substantive exchanges. No real business opportunities are discussed, no practical issues solved. So are we saying that government relations are insignificant in doing successful business in China? Not quite — but to decide on the right public affairs strategy, we must first decide what, exactly, we mean by "government relations".

3.4.2. *Which government relations do you need?*

First of all, in China as in all countries, "government" is used to denote a wide range of ministries, departments, and institutions at several levels of government — central, provincial, and local. Depending on the industry you are in, and the size of your company, all of these may impact your business.

3.4.3. *Central government*

Central government is most prominent as regulator. Some areas of business, ranging from power and infrastructure to finance, direct sales and the practice of law, are still heavily regulated. Securing permissions to do business may require extensive lobbying of central government functions.

But the central government, as well as provincial and local authorities, may also be your potential customer. In industries and projects of national significance, a government institution or state-owned enterprise may be the direct or ultimate buyer. Large corporations active in heavily regulated industries will need to build extensive relations with regulatory authorities and, of course, with government customers. But China is not unique in this respect.

In our general discussion of the guanxi concept, we have already mentioned the problems of hiring princelings, i.e. sons and daughters of high-ranking cadres, as a way of securing high-level government relations. Besides the difficulties in managing such people, it is important to consider what happens when a senior official is removed from power.

3.4.4. *Local authorities*

Local government relations, on the other hand, is the one area where most foreign businesses in China will have a real need to invest time and effort. Fostering relationships with local authorities is important because of the sometimes vague and loosely interpreted regulatory environment in China. Systems can be incomplete or patchily implemented, especially in second- and third-tier cities. Few things can be fully accomplished "by the book". Local officials are also the people who will help you out when something out of the ordinary happens. For example, China's breakneck growth has led to energy shortages in many places. Anders recalls meeting the local Party Secretary, who proceeded to call the head of the power utility in Anders' presence, saying: "General Manager Wang? Good to talk to you — we have an important foreign company on a tight production schedule and they are not getting electricity. Please call your people to make sure they get the power they need". The secretary put down the phone with a contented comment to the effect that the problem "would now soon be solved".

Such overt displays of power are not uncommon. Local functionaries are often keen to boost their own prestige in this way. Even more often, they will be incredibly friendly and helpful if you yourself have been thoughtful enough to build a good relationship ahead of time. It can be difficult to ask for a favor from an unfamiliar bureaucrat — the key is to be proactive and give face in advance by keeping in regular touch with local functionaries. Many Western businesspeople believe that such guanxi-building must take the form of endless karaoke sessions or ostentatious gift-giving, but often it is more appropriate to show ongoing respect; for example, by keeping local officials continuously informed of new business developments and plans.

Excellent government relations at the local level, with all departments related to your business is the base line: as a responsible manager, you simply must cultivate local guanxi in order to be a level player in your industry. This is not going to be a source of competitive advantage. It is just like having electricity in your factory; it is needed for production but will not ensure market success.

As the Chinese market matures, and the business environment becomes more streamlined and transparent, the need for maintaining local guanxi will also continue to decrease. But relations with local authorities such as the business and commercial bureau (which issues local business licenses), the labor bureau (hiring and firing), local environmental authorities, and state-owned utilities may still have a significant impact on day-to-day operations.

In this context, being seen as having high-level relationships with the central government may actually be useful. This is because it is a symbol of success in the status- and guanxi-driven Chinese society, and fosters a sense of concern with local authorities of antagonizing the powers that be: "He met the prime minister, what if he meets him again and tells him I could not provide electricity". In an authoritarian society, the psychology of such machinations can sometimes be important. This may indeed be one of the reasons why business people have put such inordinate efforts into arranging government-level meetings. But the effect is seldom large enough to warrant the investments made.

3.4.5. *Government relations checklist*

In summary, government relations in China may be important in some specific areas, but are often overrated:

- *There is no need to build relations for their own sake*: Central and provincial government relations, for example, are mainly significant to large corporations in heavily regulated industries. If you are in a consumer goods industry or sell industrial products to many smaller corporate customers, your need for maintaining high-level government relations will be smaller than your imperative to foster great customer relations. Do not feel guilty about avoiding the pain of organizing high-level visits with government officials just to satisfy the ego of visiting management from HQ.
- *Carefully identify the relations you really need*: Local government authorities will have an impact on smaller companies and individual subsidiaries of large corporations alike. Cultivating good relationships with local officials is a great asset in the day-to-day running of your company, especially when problems arise.
- *Create relations before you need them*: Although this is not always the case, it can be difficult to ask an unfamiliar Chinese bureaucrat for help. It may give them the impression of "being used"

or provoke them to demonstrate their power by saying "no". You should build relationships through a sustained effort well before you need to utilize them.

- *Do not overuse relations*: Most issues in modern China can be solved without resorting to high-level government relations. Save your "guanxi capital" for when you really need it.
- *Be yourself*: Western business people can go overboard in trying to behave in the way they believe is expected of them. Gifts, dinners, and other representation are sometimes necessary, but usually it is more appreciated to give "face" by keeping people informed about your thinking and plans before they demand that you do.
- *Government relations are not a business panacea*: China is a hyper-competitive market, where most companies struggle to keep up with fierce competitors. Excellent government guanxi will not guarantee that you can actually sell your products — unless the government is the direct customer, of course.

3.5. Business Etiquette

Simple business etiquette is one point of departure for practicing your face-giving and guanxi-building skills.

3.5.1. *Name cards*

The exchange of name cards is a good example. When handing over a name card, you should always use both hands — to hand it over with one hand is seen as lacking in respect for the other person. You should then subject the other person's card to detailed scrutiny, to the point of asking some question or commenting on the information on the card in some way: "I see you are responsible for the North China region — which provinces does that include?" or "Your Shanghai office is on Nanjing Road — is that far from our company's office on Jiangsu Road?" Avoid writing on the name cards of others. If you want the other party to add their mobile phone number, ask them to write it themselves.

It is alright to put the name cards of dinner guests on the table during dinner for easy referral, but do not forget to bring them with you after dinner. This advice may seem superfluous, but is actually highly pertinent because of the copious amounts of alcohol consumed during Chinese business meals.

3.5.2. *Drinking habits*

The situation has improved somewhat during recent years, and there are large differences between different regions and businesses, but in some industries, heavy drinking will still be an integral part of doing business. Toasting is systematic and organized, and aims at drinking the opposite party under the table. Johan remembers (vaguely) one of his first meetings with the Party Secretary of Bazhou, a distant Beijing suburb. The objective of trying to sell a golf training course to the local government proved elusive until the Secretary invited for a dinner at a local hotel.

Toasting started before the first dishes had been served and did not finish until the foreign visitors had been thoroughly annihilated, the host being in a state which was more difficult to determine, since he was being continuously propped up by two minions positioned each to one side of him.

Johan thought he had made a complete fool of himself, but the next day, the Secretary greeted him with a signed contract, a slap on the back and some comments to the effect that "you can only trust someone you have been dead drunk with". In some industries and social contexts in China, getting plastered is seen as a sign of respect and trustworthiness rather than a *faux pas*.[a]

3.5.3. *Table manners*

Alcohol aside, Chinese table manners are relaxed. You never have to worry about spilling sauce on the table cloth or holding your chopsticks in the wrong way. The important thing is to take care of the people around you by making sure they help themselves from every dish and that their glasses are never empty. In general, each person will use their own chopsticks to serve themselves from the dishes at the center of the table, but some hosts will even help serve their guests as an additional sign of caring and respect. In southern China, just as you should hand over name cards with both hands, you should always use both hands when pouring from a bottle for the other party, and if you are on the receiving side, you should immediately use both hands to grasp your own glass as a sign of respect. When toasting, Chinese people usually clink glasses together, and the trick is to hold the edge of your own glass lower than the edge of the person you are toasting with. As the glasses approach each other, both parties will therefore lower and tilt their glasses until they approach the surface of the table.

---

[a]For a definitive description in English of Chinese drinking habits, read Peter Hessler's delightful book *Rivertown*, which also offers one of the most perceptive general accounts of modern China that we have read.

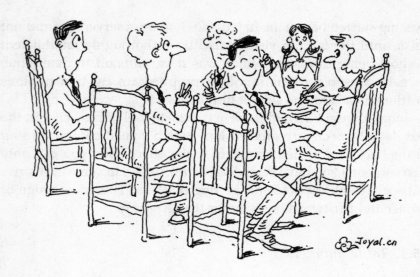

3.6. Negotiating in China

Negotiations are a part of daily business anywhere in the world. The techniques you will encounter in China are surprisingly consistent, whether you are working on a multimillion dollar contract, discussing the rental fee of your office, or trying to sell a single inexpensive product.

Jim McGregor, in his book *One Billion Customers*, provides a list of humorously provocative yet accurate insights into the Chinese negotiation process.[b] Some of his points are:

- [They] will ask you for anything, because you may just be stupid enough to agree to it. Many [foreigners] are.
- [They] always need to get concessions from you.

---

[b]Whole books have been written about negotiations in China. McGregor draws on Lucian Pye, whose book *Chinese Negotiating Style* from 1992 provides an academic summary from interviews with commercial negotiators in China. Although the social context is now somewhat dated, it remains excellent preparatory reading for anyone doing business in the country.

- Do not take what your Chinese counterpart tells you to be the truth. They will often cite rules or regulations that are non-existent just to put you in a box in working out the deal.
- China has a survival culture with a zero-sum mentality. For somebody to win, somebody has to lose.

3.6.1. *Preparation is key*

We feel that there is nothing intrinsically different about the way Chinese people negotiate as compared with those of other nationalities. Most people can be great negotiators if they are well prepared, clear on what they want to achieve, and have the advantage of a strong starting position.

Preparation is a skill that anyone can master. The challenge for the Western negotiator is mainly that the Chinese usually are really good and disciplined about preparation: they tend to do their homework on you and your position, and they know very well what they themselves want to achieve. We have, however, seen Westerners walk into negotiations in China without really knowing what to expect, and sometimes even what exactly they want to achieve. This is an unnecessary advantage given to the other side — almost as if by choice (or rather negligence).

Before starting any negotiation, it is natural to try to create a strong starting position for oneself. In some fortunate cases one may have that automatically, but in most cases it is something that has to be worked at. A strong position has to be built up well in advance of the start of the real negotiation.

To build a strong negotiating position you must first realize for yourself the value of what you have to offer and then make sure that your counterpart also understands it. We have represented different companies in negotiations with Chinese companies and authorities. It is amazing the difference it makes in negotiating power, if you represent a big and well-known company (like Sandvik in metal cutting) compared to a small not so well-known company.

In a negotiation with a Chinese counterpart, this is not so easy, because they often have something that the Westerner really does want, namely access to the "huge Chinese market". If that is indeed what the Western businessman is after, then the Chinese counterpart is certainly in a strong starting position. Western businessmen tend to help them create this strong position through their own expectations. This is certainly enjoyable for the Chinese counterpart and there is little we can do about it. Potential is a currency of sorts — and one that, despite repeated disappointments, has kept foreigners lined up at China's gate throughout history.

3.6.2. *Do not take "truths" at face value*

Preparation should include an in-depth assessment of regulations and market conditions that will influence the negotiations. Chinese negotiators will ruthlessly exploit foreign cluelessness by inventing rules or customs that work in their own favor. What is culturally acceptable differs from country to country; what a Western businessman might see as "misrepresenting the facts" may not be seen as morally reprehensible in a Chinese business situation: "surely, it must be up to the other party to check the facts that they want to trust". For a taste of this aspect of Chinese business, just visit a market in any city in the country. You will be offered polyester scarves marked "100% pure silk", and cotton shirts made of nylon. Prices will vary by a factor of ten or more, depending on your skills as a negotiator.

Still, beware of overestimating the deviousness of the other party. Do not discount the possibility that misunderstandings in the discussions stem from *bona fide* confusion and lack of business experience on the other side. At one time, Anders was looking at purchasing a state-owned company. Anders noticed on the organization chart that the company's quality department reported to the finance department. "This looks strange", Anders said, "can it really be correct?" A loud and engaged discussion erupted between the representatives of the acquisition target. After a few minutes, one of them went for a pair of scissors and some glue and proceeded to cut out the quality department from its place as part of the financial department and put it under production instead, asking if Anders was happier with the new arrangement. "Well, you at least seem to have an admirably flexible organization", Anders noted.

As previously, due diligence and a correct assessment of the other party's real capabilities is crucial. A good friend in the furniture business ordered several containers of office chair parts from a local manufacturer, only to discover that the supplier was unable to meet the technical specifications. It turned out that the poor guy had been so afraid of losing the business that he had fabricated nonexistent technical capabilities even though it had been obvious even to himself that he would ultimately be unable to meet the required specifications.

3.6.3. *Identify your own strengths*

Western negotiators tend to underestimate what they bring to the table; they may want market access, but the Chinese side is looking for something as well, often capital and/or technology. A good starting position comes from a full appreciation of our own strengths.

A useful internal exercise at an early stage is therefore to ask oneself: What does the other party really want to get from us? By putting ourselves in their shoes, we can make ourselves more aware of our strengths and thereby market them a lot better. In negotiations for bigger deals, where your counterpart has shown serious interest and is preparing for negotiations, it may be worthwhile to invite them to a well-planned study tour to the parent company, where you can demonstrate technological advantages and show the latest investments. You need to be at the stage where negotiations are imminent — otherwise, such a visit can easily become a paid vacation. The objective is to enhance your negotiation position by impressing and building interest in a casual way, rather than a "hard sell" of your advantages. In the negotiations, it is essential that these cards are played well and not given away too easily.

Remember that China is a huge country, with many players. Westerners tend to be so focused on getting results that we regard walking away from an agreement as a failure. But there will always be other opportunities than the one you are presently pursuing. By avoiding to agree too easily, you often earn the chance to come back and negotiate again later (or to negotiate with somebody else) and then achieving a better result.

3.6.4. *Time pressure*

Handling time pressure is an oft-repeated challenge in Chinese negotiations. Anders had, in agreement with the counterpart, allocated two days for a negotiation in the medium-sized Chinese city of Xi'an and was booked on a flight back to Beijing on the second day. "We would certainly be ready by then and probably have some time to look at some local historic sites as well" was the statement. After the first day of negotiations and a traditional banquet, Anders's reflection was that his counterpart was not really interested in speeding up the negotiations. It was hard to avoid the conclusion that they wanted to put us into a time trap. Unknown to them (through our office in Beijing) we therefore changed our departure until mid-day the following day and with rooms booked in another hotel. The second day of negotiations started and in the afternoon it was time to start to come to decisions. Our counterpart tried to rush us into a less favorable agreement pointing out that we had to leave soon to catch our flight. He became very disturbed, when we declared that we had changed our bookings until the following day. The leader of their delegation was personally unhappy, since he had to leave for a meeting with his boss that evening to report on the result of the negotiations. We quickly reached an agreement.

3.6.5. *Work cultural differences to your advantage*

McGregor points out that the Chinese preoccupation with face, for example, can play to a foreigner's advantage: "If the talks meet an impasse caused by the Chinese side, it is easy for the foreigner to take the blame and move discussions ahead. You also lose nothing by treating even the most obnoxious Chinese negotiator with exaggerated respect. Treat him or her with the inflated importance they expect, but look out for your own bottom line. Engage in the theatrics, but don't let it slide over into substance".

Compare the bargaining about price in a Chinese market. The more patient you are, the less you pay. The Chinese tend to be tenacious negotiators. Do not be so impatient that you give up your position too early and too easily. The more eager you are, the more you will give up (often unnecessarily).

None of the above — preparations, clear objectives, advance positioning, and patience — are specific to negotiations in China. They are just as valid in the West, though in our experience Chinese negotiators tend to be disciplined in their delivery on these points. And foreign businessmen seem to forget these basic principles as soon as they set foot on Chinese soil.

3.6.6. *Dealing with hierarchy*

There is, however, one major difference between negotiations in China and most Western countries. In China, it is almost always difficult to get a direct negotiation with the ultimate decision maker. The mandate on the Chinese side is often "to negotiate", which is quite different from the mandate for the Western party, which is usually "to reach an agreement" (within certain parameters). In most negotiations in China, the Chinese side needs to go back and discuss with someone higher up before finally accepting any result of a negotiation. This is regarded as legitimate, indeed perfectly natural, but it has two unfortunate consequences for the Western counterpart. Not knowing whether one has actually reached agreement or not can be frustrating. What is more, having to go back for confirmation also means the Chinese party will often return to the discussions wanting to renegotiate certain parts of the agreement, using the preliminary agreement as a baseline and expecting to continue moving their own position forward.

Let us say you are asking your Chinese counterpart for concessions on X, Y, and Z. They, on their hand, would like you to agree to A, B, and C. In your discussions, you do indeed agree to two of these points, A and B, provided they agree to X and Y. They then declare that they need approval from their decision maker and come back from these internal consultations stating that "our manager is OK with X and Y, but only if you give in on C as well". Typically, they would then expect the discussion to focus on C exclusively — after all, you already agreed to A and B. Should you give in on point C as well, it would not be uncommon for them to feel encouraged to come back with a new, previously unstated, demand D that they "just had not thought of before"!

The harried Western businessman, for whom time is money, has no simple solution to this problem. But there is one method that has worked well in practice for us: stating as a principle the mutual right to renegotiate any preliminary agreement if the other party changes its position, and then sticking to this principle in an unwavering, consequent fashion.

Here is how it works: At the outset of negotiations, declare clearly that if you offer certain concessions to reach a "preliminary agreement" and your counterparts want to go back to discuss these internally, then you will not regard your position on any particular point as fixed if they want to renegotiate other points. In other words, if both parties preliminarily agree, but your counterparts get pushback from their ultimate decision maker, they can expect that you may change other aspects of your position. This means — crucially — that if they want continued discussions (read renegotiation), you are not going to start negotiating from the position of the preliminary agreement, but from the original position you had at the outset of negotiations.

In other words, using the hypothetical scenario above, when your counterparts come back demanding to discuss C, you then reiterate your principle that the previous agreement on points A and B is null and void, and consequently ask to renegotiate all three points A, B, and C from scratch.

A declaration like this does not alter the Chinese side's fundamental need to take matters home for consultations. It does, however, tend to neutralize the related advantages by making them more careful in demanding endless renegotiations, since they have no guarantee that the preliminarily reached positions will be attained again.

We see this technique as a way to negate an unfair advantage in negotiation style. But when initially confronted with these ground rules, the Chinese side often actually tends to see them as unfair; they are used to having the unilateral right to come back for renegotiation of a preliminary agreement. For the technique to work, it is therefore essential that your principles are clearly explained and understood at the outset of discussions and continuously reinforced throughout.

Being aware of the Chinese counterpart's need to consult with and persuade the ultimate decision maker can also help you smooth the negotiation process in another way. Your counterpart will need to take back to his or her decision maker clearly stated arguments for the rationale of concessions; you must furnish and explain these arguments to make them persuasive when relayed to "head office". It is therefore good practice to support your counterpart with written notes or detailed oral summaries of the reasons for your stated position to make sure they are accurately transmitted.

3.6.7. *Leveraging the trust advantage*

The reason guanxi, doing business with people you know, is so important in China, is precisely because Chinese business people build their trust on such personal networks. But by default, foreign companies and brands are actually often more trusted than local ones, even to the extent that local companies have tried to choose foreign-sounding names or made themselves into joint ventures (with a Hong-Kong listed subsidiary as the "foreign" party). Although this advantage is being gradually eroded as Chinese companies become world-class competitors, it is still worth exploiting.

Anders remembers negotiating rental contracts for offices in second-tier Chinese cities in the 1990s. There were sometimes no real office buildings in these places at that time, so offices were made by renting a number of ordinary hotel rooms and then connecting them by making internal doors or openings. The major modifications to entire hotel floors made for interesting negotiations, during which playing the card of International Company worked well. Although the belief was that foreign companies had deeper pockets than local tenants, Anders actually managed to get cheaper rents than most local neighbors in this way. First, his Chinese colleagues would use their local networks of contacts to establish a benchmark of what local companies were paying in a particular location. After a few rounds of discussions we would usually reach a price at, or slightly above, this "local" level, but below this price, negotiations started becoming more difficult. At this stage, Anders would systematically play "the trust card", emphasizing that as a multinational company, he was required to always pay bills on time. In almost every city, this gave an extra 5–10% lower price after internal discussions on the landlord's side.

Trust becomes even more essential in difficult times. If you take care of employees during a recession, instead of just letting them go, you will get a high loyalty bonus from your local colleagues. During the financial turmoil of late 2008 and early 2009, "safe employment" became a major positive factor for retention. This was not usually the case before the financial crisis, but we believe it will be remembered during better times.

In general, we have found that foreign companies, especially large companies with strong brands, have a major advantage over local companies when it comes to trust in China. Foreign companies are held to higher standards than local companies, and must demonstrate that they live up to these expectations even in times of difficulties. But if you continue to demonstrate that you are a trustworthy business partner, this can be a competitive advantage and give you strong leverage in negotiations.

3.6.8. *Checklist for successful negotiations in China*

*   *Do your homework*: The phrase from Sun Zi's *Art of War* that Chinese people most like to quote is: "if you understand your enemy and you understand yourself, you will win all battles".

- *Understand the framework within which discussions will take place*: Is there a time factor involved?
- *Try to put yourself in the shoes of your counterpart*: What are the key advantages he would like to gain? What are you bringing to the table? How urgent is agreement to him?
- *Be clear on what you want*: Prepare scenarios and set limits on how much you are prepared to give on every parameter in the discussions.
- *Be patient*: Never put yourself under time pressure — it will be ruthlessly exploited by your counterpart.
- *Set the framework*: State in clear and unequivocal terms your right to always renegotiate from scratch if the Chinese party claims pushback on certain points of preliminarily reached agreements.
- *Provide rationale for purchase*: Help your counterpart explain to home office decision makers the rationale behind your arguments.

Chapter 4
The Language Challenge

In 2000, Johan attended a management meeting of a Fortune-500 company in Beijing. The company had just gone through a major restructuring, much of the old management had been removed, and the new Country Manager felt it appropriate to "address the troops" as soon as possible upon arrival. Being British, this manager is an excellent speaker with a real gift for rhetorical flourishes. He outlined the challenges, suggested the overall direction of solutions, and expressed his confidence in the (remaining) management. Given the importance of the moment, his speech waxed gradually more eloquent as he approached the finale: "So, colleagues, how will we know that we have succeeded in China? Let me tell you. We will know that we have succeeded in China when our manufacturing is the industry leader in quality. We will know that we have succeeded in China, when our Company's product is the top-of-mind choice for Chinese consumers. And we will know that we have succeeded in China when every month, you get a call from a headhunter offering you a 30% higher salary, and you still choose to stay with our Company rather than take that offer".

Then came the translation: "So, do you believe that we will succeed in China? Do you believe that our product can be the top quality choice for Chinese consumers? If you do not believe that, and a headhunter offers you a 30% higher salary, then let me tell you this, right now: you should rather take that offer than stay with our Company".

The audience mulled over this information while waiting for the next translation as their new manager went on to say: "Now: as managers, what do I want you to tell your people when you leave this room? I want you to tell them to believe in the future of our Company. I want you to tell them that we are committed to success in China. I want you to tell them we will win on this market. Thank you".

What the assembled coworkers heard was this: "Now, if anyone doesn't want to tell their people to believe in the future or our Company and our success in China, I want you to leave this room, right now".

At this point, Johan found it pertinent to jump on stage and explain more accurately to the shell-shocked Chinese managers what their new boss had actually said.

4.1. Language is and will Remain an Issue

Few people in China speak really good English. Even those who sound reasonably proficient will often misunderstand more subtle points. For a manager who does not speak Chinese, this presents obvious challenges. One of the most severe is that you will not be able to "address the troops" orally in their own language. You will only be able to communicate with a select group who in turn must communicate it onward. This will influence many aspects of day-to-day business: in a sales organization, it becomes more difficult to speak to the customers; during negotiations, extraordinary care must be spent making sure you really understand what your counterpart means, and so on. If you use humor as a management and communications tool, make sure the joke is so simple that the translator can understand it. Humor depends heavily on cultural context and linguistic subtleties. This makes translation so difficult for Chinese interpreters that most jokes simply end up being left out of translations, leaving the manager to wonder why no-one ever laughs in China.

Most importantly, the language barrier tends to limit the flow of information from the workforce to yourself; in any organization, employees tend to limit the flow of information to the management, but the consequences become especially pronounced in China.

If you do not speak Chinese, you will have to work through an interpreter. Your interpreter will also face challenges. Some are rooted in the structure of the language: Chinese uses 10,000 as the basic unit of calculations instead of the 1,000 used in the West. "One million" is expressed as "a hundred ten-thousands" and "a hundred million" as "ten thousand ten-thousands". This is of course a total nightmare for translators, whose key strength, in China as elsewhere, was never arithmetic.

Other challenges stem from a failure to understand the cultural context and frame of reference of the foreigner. Many industries are new to China and you cannot be certain that your Chinese colleagues share your experiences. Subjective issues are therefore easily confused; try asking your counterpart the same question several times on separate occasions, and you will be surprised by how different the answers can be.

Cultural issues, such as a preoccupation with face, can also play a role in translation. Chinese translators sometimes avoid interrupting the flow to go back and ask questions about specific terms that they do not understand.

4.2. Make Sure Your Interpreter Understands the Business

Managing the language challenge depends on having access to excellent translation in all business situations. As we have seen, controlling the quality of translations can be difficult. But there are some ways of minimizing the language problem:

- *Ensure quality*: Make sure you have a proficient interpreter; if in doubt, replace him immediately. In a negotiation, always bring your own colleague to do translation.
- *Keep the interpreter in the loop*: Try to include your interpreter in business discussions even on occasions where there is no need for translation, so that he is clear about the rationale for what

you are trying to communicate. It is important that you know the translator well and that he/she knows you well too. We tend to "mean more than we say" — translation quality improves tremendously if the interpreter has a good understanding of the background and context of what is being said.

- *Prepare in advance*: On important issues, always brief your interpreter well in advance on the main points of what you are going to say.
- *Support with written material*: As a reference for the interpreter, always write down figures, especially large ones, in advance.
- *Do not ramble*: Speak slowly and clearly in short, easily translated "sound bites".
- *Be as concrete as possible*: Avoid rhetoric and poetic language.
- *Be careful with humor*: Wit is difficult to translate, especially for an interpreter who does not share the speaker's sense of humor.
- *Assume that others may understand you when you may not want to be understood*: Remember (especially if your native language is English) that just because you need an interpreter, that does not mean you have a secret language. Count on the possibility that somebody on the other side will actually be well versed in your own language, but may not say so because of lack of confidence — or a desire to pick up any asides you may be having with your own team.
- *If you speak Chinese, you should not necessarily enlighten your counterpart to the fact that you do*: Your counterpart may assume that because you need an interpreter, you do not understand the language. This can sometimes work to your advantage.

4.3. Beware of the "Confidant Trap"

While it is important that the interpreter has a deep understanding of your business, you must be careful to make sure your "interpreter" does not start negotiating on your behalf. It is not infrequent to hear translators who start investing their own ideas into the discussion, rather than just translating. This is an example of a more general problem which has been called the "confidant trap".

In a 2004 article in the Harvard Business Review, workplace psychologist Kerry J. Sulkowicz describes the unhealthy relationships that can easily develop between what he calls the "CEO's confidant" and the CEO. Sulkowicz highlights the negative consequences: the confidant tends to become a filter on reality and can easily limit the manager's access to other parts of the organization.

We have seen several such negative relationships develop in China. The confidant, whose English skills are often his or her only competitive advantage within the organization, can become territorial about access to and communication with the boss. Information is filtered and interpreted to the exclusion of important information. In serious cases, the confidant usurps important decisions from the manager.

Most Country Managers are men, and almost all secretaries are women. Most of the time, managers will be able to handle themselves well, but even when the relationship is just *seen* as being too close, it can still lead to complications in the form of rumors and an even greater distancing of the manager from the overall organization.

In some organizations, the playing field becomes more generally skewed towards coworkers who can "talk the talk" — who, by dint of excellent verbal skills and an MBA degree, can use the right terminology and thus give the impression of understanding and strategic thinking. In an environment where the PowerPoint slides of other colleagues sometimes become unintelligible due to mundane issues of grammar and vocabulary, it is easy to overestimate those who can express themselves clearly. Peter Humphrey, one of China's most experienced risk management consultants, now heading his own consultancy ChinaWhys, comments that "often head office or a senior expatriate manager... over-rely on a single point of reporting — usually a local hire with good English — to provide them with information about the operation. This person gathers power and controls the whole business: language, connections to the government, internal networks, external social networks, direct contact with suppliers, direct contact with distributors, and loyalty from other staff within the company".

The so-called "haigui" or "sea turtles" pose a particular problem. The term, which denotes Chinese nationals returning to China after work or studies abroad, is a play on the Chinese word for sea, "hai", which also means "overseas", and turtle, "gui", which is pronounced the same as "return". Haigui are often highly educated and culture-savvy, having been educated abroad, but fresh "turtles" lack on-the-ground experience and crucial networks. It will therefore take them a few years to adapt back to the Chinese business environment. They also frequently develop a temporary superiority complex from their own unique experiences, which can cause friction with local coworkers.

Remember that Chinese returnees and MBA students who speak excellent English may lack the work experience and implementation skills that are the most critical prerequisites to success in the Chinese day-to-day environment. The Chinese business world is cluttered with verbal, suave English speakers who contribute little to, or sometimes even detract from, the companies they are working for. What you really need is experienced people, or, barring that, youthful talent to develop from scratch.

4.4. Checklist for Non-Chinese Speakers

Managers learn to live with most of these problems. Here is our checklist for managers who do not speak Chinese:

- *Be aware*: The language issue is more fundamental than you may suspect. Linguistic fluency does not guarantee cultural or contextual understanding.
- *Emphasize written communications*: Writing important communications down makes it easier to ensure correct translation — and gives you an extra chance to rehash your messages as well.

- *Get a great translator — but not a proxy*: Managers need to have access to perfect translation and this can only come by bringing the translator close to the business and close to yourself. But do not allow the relationship to develop into an unhealthy dependency.
- *Do not overestimate candidates with good language skills or MBA's*: When recruiting and promoting, look for potential, shared values, and a good "gut feeling" rather than glitzy presentation.

Chapter 5

Qualities of the Right Expatriate Manager

In our experience, most multinational headquarters are not aware of the great potential for developing international talent in China by exposing them to a different and challenging business environment; instead, they staff their China operations from the perspective of running the local business. China is usually not yet valued as an asset for corporate experience. This will probably change as China operations continue to grow and become more important for companies, but the opportunity is already here.

International managers that we talked to mentioned speed, hunger, and can-do attitude; a heightened awareness of costs; and patience and tolerance as some key skills and attributes that they have gleaned from their China experience. Ian Duffy of IKEA summarized this by saying "After a while in China, nothing seems to faze you. This is a more volatile environment than other markets where I have worked — anything could happen on a day-to-day basis. You learn to think on your feet in order to adapt". The same thing is true for individuals as for companies: if you can succeed in China, you can probably succeed anywhere.

5.1. Send Your Best People

One important lesson we can learn from successful companies is that they send their best — in the sense of "most suited" — people to China. In the 1990s, no matter how its potential was getting hyped, China was still a small, faraway niche market for most companies. This often meant that companies would send those managers to China who were not senior or capable enough to handle "more important" markets in the USA or Europe. Lack of management talent led to many, perhaps even most, of the failures that companies experienced in the Chinese market.

Successful companies, on the other hand, said: "Starting and founding a new business is never easy and China seems like an especially challenging place — can we find someone in our existing worldwide organization who is capable and experienced enough to handle these challenges, someone with the right personality for building a business and who will be excited about developing the local organization?"

Some companies believed that they would need a local manager, or at least a Chinese speaker from Hong Kong, Taiwan, or Singapore, in order to succeed in China. In many cases, this was a recipe for disaster. Not only did these managers lack the necessary understanding of the company's culture as well as contacts and support at head office; they often encountered as large, or larger, culture shock as their Western counterparts. Hong Kong managers, in particular, were known for being condescending and lacking respect for mainland employees; this, however, seems to have improved as we enter the 21st century.

More and more, multinationals will be competing with local companies not only for the top local talent, but also for expatriates with Chinese business experience. Shanghai Automotive Industry Corp (SAIC), the mainland's largest car company, hired Phil Murtaugh, a General Motors veteran who used to head up GM in China, as head of its international operations. Lenovo appointed Bill Amelio, the American head of Asia-Pacific for Dell Computer, as chief executive. And these are just the most high-profile cases in a larger trend.

China also offers a great opportunity for multinationals to train the leaders of the future. If China offers a glimpse of the future business environment in a globalized world, giving the best and brightest a chance to hone their management skills in the extreme competition and fast pace of the local market can be rewarding to the whole organization.

In their book *China CEO*, Fernandez and Underwood divide the requisite qualities of the ideal expatriate China manager into three categories: "Professional", "personal global", and "personal China-specific" qualities.

5.2. Professional Qualities

In our experience, most successful companies send out managers who have been with the company for a long time, are well steeped in the culture and have strong established networks within the worldwide organization.

There are several reasons for this:

- *It bridges the distance with head office*: Having a good informal network inside the worldwide organization provides access to information and support.
- *It allows the manager to act as a role model*: An in-depth understanding of the corporate culture allows the manager to act unambiguously and become a strong role model for local employees.
- *It makes the manager into a good ambassador for the company*: In China, the local manager will represent the company in dealing with business partners and government authorities; familiarity with one's own company culture and industry exudes self-confidence and builds trust.

Ideally, the candidate should also have experience from working outside his or her home country. Adjusting to a new country is always an effort and can sometimes be debilitating, especially when the cultural and social differences are as large as those between China and the West. In-depth understanding of the company combined with international experience are therefore the requisite "professional qualities".

5.3. Personal Qualities

You should also try to choose a personality that suits what you are trying to accomplish in China. Your local manager needs to be humble and respectful of the local culture, yet assertive enough to take decisions and make sure the organization sticks with these decisions. Avoid "loud" expatriates with all the answers, people who come to China to sell the locals on their own way of doing business. Instead, choose good listeners who take pride in mentoring and supporting young, ambitious people. In our opinion, the ideal candidate can often be described as "ambitious and aggressive, yet friendly".

China is exciting, intriguing, and exotic. It is the golden land of opportunity. But it is also frequently dirty, noisy, rude, and chaotic. Only someone who is genuinely curious about the country, its culture, and people, someone who really wants to experience China, will find the energy to overcome the challenges of working in such a different, and sometimes exasperating, environment.

This inquisitiveness or curiosity is what Fernandez and Underwood call the personal global qualities of "multicultural mindset" and "commitment to learn". To this they add the personal China-specific qualities of "humility, strength, patience and speed".

Patience and persistence are perhaps the most critical personality traits for the expatriate manager. China will test your patience in a myriad of ways, from trying to penetrate the convoluted regulatory environment and waiting for approvals and licenses to nurturing and developing your local organization.

Humility means being able to accept that China is a unique business environment and that global corporate strategies have to be locally adapted. This humility, however, has to be tempered by integrity. Local colleagues will see her or him as a role model. Balancing global corporate culture and local business practices is one of the most challenging jobs for any expatriate manager in China. Again, having a solid background in the worldwide organization helps tremendously in this area.

Your expatriate manager must be particularly strong in coaching skills. As we will see, your Chinese organization will usually be less mature than that of other countries, so management must be ready to coach younger and greener colleagues.

Speed is not the opposite of patience — it is about moving forward and being able to take quick decisions in the face of change. Chinese business people are often distressed by the tectonic pace of decision making at foreign companies. In an environment as fast-moving and fluid as that of China, the local manager must act decisively to take the opportunities that appear.

As we have seen, Chinese managers are generally better than Westerners at relating personally to their coworkers. In order to build loyalty with Chinese coworkers and nurture a strong team allowing him to succeed in China, the expatriate manager therefore needs to have great soft skills in management. He must also enjoy building networks and relationships with external constituents: business partners, government agencies, etc. Do not send someone to a senior posting in China unless he or she is a real "people person".

5.4. Long-Term Commitment

A successful candidate should be prepared to stay for at least four years, preferably longer. One of the major complaints from Chinese employees is the lack of constancy in business strategy which stems from frequent management changes. Companies who change their expatriate managers frequently tend to lose their best local employees more frequently as well. In knowledge-intensive industries such as consulting, this can make or break the business. Take the PR industry as an example: All of the top-20 major multinational agencies are present in China, but there is a clear line of demarcation between the market leaders, who continue to grow above average, and the laggards. All of the high-growth agencies are headed by managers who have spent many years with the local organization.

Long-term commitment is important for building external relations as well. Ian Duffy, Manager of IKEA in Asia-Pacific, recalls being given some friendly advice by a Chinese government official: "In my government job, I meet Western managers all the time. We meet and exchange friendly greetings and empty phrases with no follow-up. If I am going to trust and work with somebody, it is because they come back to me and maintain a long-term relationship. Credibility comes with time; it is not just personal qualities that are important".

It is also a good idea to take a holistic look at the candidate's family situation. A supportive family (or at least the absence of a not so supportive family) can be a huge asset for an expatriate manager. The Chinese business environment can be demanding: long work hours combined with spending your time in a foreign environment 7 days a week, 24 hours a day. It is a good idea to interview the person's family, and to involve them early in the career decision of whether to go to China.

Chapter 6

Company Setup

If the newly arrived manager is tasked with setting up or restructuring the Chinese operations of the company, he will be faced with a number of choices:

- location
- legal structure
- business partners to involve in manufacturing, distribution, marketing, etc.
- consultants, lawyers, and other professional service providers.

Let us look at each of these in turn.

6.1. Geographic Considerations

China's size makes the choice of location for offices and manufacturing facilities of paramount importance. Some companies chose specific locations for special reasons such as the presence of business or joint-venture partners, access to raw materials, etc. But most companies locate their head offices in either of the three major cities Beijing, Shanghai, or Hong Kong more or less by default. What are some of the considerations for and against each of these locations?

6.1.1. *Beijing*

During the 1980s and 1990s, Beijing was the destination of choice for most multinational head offices. The features that made the capital attractive then still hold true today:

- *Proximity to government institutions*: China's government is centralized, with all key government functions located in Beijing. This is particularly important for companies with government customers, for example in the infrastructure and IT industries.

- *Access to academic institutions*: Beijing is more than politics; it is also the education and research capital of China, with over a hundred universities and many research institutes providing abundant access to qualified recruits and research partnerships.

However, there are also drawbacks:

- *Environment*: Although the situation has improved after the 2008 Olympics Beijing is still more polluted than, for example, Shanghai, with notorious dust storms affecting air quality especially during the early spring months. A redeeming feature is the nearby, sparsely populated mountain areas which are excellent for hiking, skiing and other outdoor activities.
- *Traffic*: There has been little effort to manage the rapid access to cars by the affluent middle class. The result has been incessant traffic jams which waste enormous amounts of time and make it difficult to plan meetings. Most senior Beijing business people hire drivers, allowing them to work in the car.
- *Red tape*: Beijing is also the bureaucratic capital of China.
- *Parochialism*: Although there is a large expatriate community from multinational corporations, embassies and international organizations, Beijing still lacks the international atmosphere of cities like Hong Kong and Shanghai.

6.1.2. *Shanghai*

During the first years of the 21st century, Shanghai overtook Beijing as the main magnet for foreign companies. Although the expatriate community is not yet as large as those of Beijing or Hong Kong, it is growing and has reached the critical mass where schools and other facilities are abundant. Shanghai also boasts a number of other business attractions:

- *Convenient location*: Shanghai sits in the middle of China, making it convenient for companies with pan-Chinese operations.

- *Excellent transportation*: An excellent sea port, two airports, and the central location make Shanghai a convenient hub. International connections are good and improving.
- *Efficient local authorities*: In Shanghai, perhaps more than anywhere else in China, rules and regulations are clear, reasonably transparent and effectively implemented.

The main drawbacks are:

- *High-costs*: Almost everything, from office rent to hotels and restaurants, is more expensive in Shanghai. Office rents in the early 2000s were at mid-Manhattan levels.
- *Soaring wages and a shortage of qualified personnel*: Shanghai labor costs are rapidly approaching international levels. For experienced managers, expect to pay as much as, or more than, in developed countries.
- *Extreme urbanization*: Shanghai is a huge, sprawling city which merges into the surrounding suburbs and satellite cities. In order to get access to anything resembling natural countryside, you will need to travel for a couple of hours to nearby Hangzhou.

6.1.3. *Hong Kong and Guangzhou*

Multinational companies have traditionally located their Asian or even China headquarters in Hong Kong. Today, however, Hong Kong is often seen as a legacy location for multinational companies, at least in manufacturing and consumer goods (the financial industry, however, remains stronger in Hong Kong than in mainland cities like Shanghai). Many companies had existing organizations, partners or agencies in Hong Kong, which, as the Chinese market opened up in the 1980s and 1990s, were gradually tasked with expanding into China.

The attractions of Hong Kong include:

- *Rule of law and status as a Special Administrative Region*: Hong Kong's mature legal infrastructure, which is modeled on

British law, make it attractive compared to the more fluid mainland environment.

- *Multicultural and multilingual environment*: As a former British Crown Colony, Hong Kong is by far the most cosmopolitan city of China.
- *High standard of service and infrastructure*: In Hong Kong, everything just works. The subway system is the envy of most cities.
- *Ready access to Western goods at reasonable prices*: Hong Kong has a long history of catering to cosmopolitan tastes and does not levy customs duties or VAT.
- *China's only international finance centre with a fully convertible currency, the Hong Kong Dollar*: Hong Kong is therefore the China hub for financial institutions with satellite offices in Shanghai, Beijing, and other Chinese cities.
- *Beautiful natural environment*: Hong Kong comprises pristine forests and hiking areas.

If standard of living were the only consideration, most companies would still locate their China headquarters to Hong Kong. The international heritage and special status of the city, however, are also its main drawback: it is more difficult to succeed in China from a distance, even if the distance is as short as that between Hong Kong and Shenzhen in Southern China.

Some companies remain in Hong Kong, although it would probably make more business sense for the China headquarters to be located close to the market it oversees, especially since the growth of mainland business has often dwarfed the original Hong Kong operations. Personal reasons — the established lifestyle of expatriate and Hong Kong-Chinese business people, where the kids go to established schools and spouses enjoy a comfortable life — have delayed the decisions of companies to move operations to mainland China. Such reluctance is increasingly being overruled by savvy head offices.

Guangzhou remains the headquarters of a few large multinational companies like Procter & Gamble, but fewer new Western companies seem to be establishing themselves in this part of China.

6.1.4. *Other cities*

For some companies, it makes sense to establish operations in other Chinese cities than those mentioned above. But there are certain considerations to be taken into account when deciding to go beyond the beaten path:

- *Possibility to attract expatriate, and possibly local, employees*: Cities like Suzhou and Hangzhou close to Shanghai and Tianjin nearby Beijing have large expatriate communities and good facilities, but it is sometimes difficult to find and retain managers who are willing to live with the cultural isolation and lack of material comforts of smaller cities located farther from major urban centers.
- *Laxer implementation of regulations*: The Chinese saying "the mountains are high and the emperor far away" alludes to the fact that the further one gets from the main developed cities, the more powerful local authorities will be. Due diligence becomes more complicated the further you move from Beijing.
- *Transportation and logistics*: We have worked with several companies where transportation costs have proven an insurmountable long-term obstacle to company's development. These companies were often forced into joint ventures with local competitors and therefore established operations at the partner's location. In one case, a Fortune-500 multinational bought into a large factory conveniently located by a railroad connection, where local authorities also promised to provide transportation subsidies to compensate for the inland location while waiting for canal works to lower transportation costs. The railroad turned out to pass through People's Liberation Army territory on its way to the factory and was therefore off-grounds to commercial interests, and

the transportation subsidies dried up after changes in the city leadership.

6.2. Development Zones

All major cities in China will boast dedicated "development zones". Some of these hundreds of zones are "high-tech" or dedicated to a certain industry, others are customs-free enclaves for assembly and re-export of products. Depending on type, they offer preferential treatment in any number of areas, including:

- *Land use*: Zones may offer relatively inexpensive land with ready-made infrastructure and clear land use rights.
- *Excellent service*: Most zones offer some kind of "one-stop-shopping" facilities that handle registration and licensing with the multitude of government bureaucracies that would otherwise have to be handled one by one: the tax bureau, commercial and industrial bureau, environmental bureau, and so on.
- *Registration and licensing*: Some types of foreign-owned enterprises have only been possible to register in designated zones.
- *Tax policy*: Zones may offer tax breaks, deferred payments, or end-of-year tax reimbursements.

When dealing with smaller zones, it is important to realize that the central government has clear regulations for which preferential treatments are and are not allowed. Zones compete fiercely for investment and may offer illegal incentives to lure investors. This has cost some companies dearly when the central government has intervened and rolled back incentives that were promised locally.

6.3. Legal Structure

The type of enterprise that foreigners have been able to establish in China has changed over the years. Below, we will recap some of the most common business models and discuss in depth some of the more attractive ones.

6.3.1. *Representative office*

Many companies started their China businesses by establishing a so-called representative office, or "rep office" for short. This office was the China arm of the overseas parent company or one of its subsidiaries, typically the company registered in Hong Kong. A rep office could only *represent* its parent company, it was not allowed to do any direct business itself. For example, it was not allowed to advertise or to invoice for goods or services rendered.

The role of a rep office was therefore limited to liaising between the Chinese buyer (or rather its "export/import company", since trade was the oligopoly of a handful of state-owned trading companies) and the parent company. Invoicing and delivery was handled directly by the parent company and the Chinese customer paid the parent company directly, usually through a bank with a letter of credit.

Taxation is one of the major drawbacks of a representative office. Since the rep office cannot, by definition, do business or invoice for goods or services rendered, it is instead taxed on the volume of its expenses. This can make it expensive to maintain a larger organization.

Today, rep offices have become rarer, but they are still useful in a few cases:

- *As an inexpensive start-up*: The set up of a representative office is relatively hassle-free and there are no demands on registered capital being transferred into the country.
- *When business volume will be small*: If the size of your business does not warrant the capital needed to start a corporate entity, a rep office can be relatively inexpensive.
- *When activities are off-limits to international firms*: Law-firms, for example, are not allowed to practice in China, and so do their

work through representative offices that in turn hire services from local firms.

6.3.2. *Joint venture*

If a company wants to make a larger commitment to its investment in China, for example by starting manufacturing, it needs to register a formal corporate entity. In the 1980s and early 1990s, this was usually done in the form of a joint venture with a local partner. In some industries, this was actually the only form of legal structure allowed to foreign firms; this remains the case today for some business areas such as telecom and automotive.

There are remarkable success stories, where thoughtful structuring, realistic objectives, and careful handling of mutual relations in a respectful way have lead to fruitful, sustainable, and profitable partnerships: multinationals have created such JV's in the car industry, in telecom, in aircraft maintenance, and other areas.

In some heavily regulated industries, foreign companies are not allowed to establish independent organizations and are therefore relegated to arranged marriages with Chinese state-owned enterprises.

Today, there is a lot of disillusionment with the joint-venture model. Companies that do have a choice tend to avoid the joint-venture model since it adds complexity that will often slow down momentum and short-term business progress and prevent the organization from building a constructive long-term corporate culture.

By and large, JV's tend to be problematic. There have been lots of books written about the most spectacular joint-venture failures such as Chrysler's cooperation with Beijing Jeep. But there were also many (at least theoretical) advantages of forming a joint venture: for example, immediate access to a manufacturing operation and established sales and distribution network, and excellent contacts with local authorities and customers. The initial costs are lower than for a green field operation, since the local partner will often contribute land (land use rights), buildings, and machinery into the joint venture. The biggest perceived disadvantage was the risk of technology and know-how leaking into the Chinese partner's company.

In some cases, this threat actually did become reality. In the end, multinationals ended up providing technology, processes, and other intellectual property that enabled the "partner" to set up a competing business.

In our work, we once encountered a forced restructuring of a major production JV in China. Sales were slack and the financials were deteriorating — what could be done to revive the business? It was quickly discovered that the lackluster financial performance was only a symptom of more serious problems. It turned out that the Chinese partner had set up a factory to produce products that were nearly identical with those produced by the JV — except that prices were much lower. Sales staff at the local partner were proudly announcing to prospective customers that their product offering had been produced using "the same technology" as those of the JV.

This case illustrates some common issues with JV's. Most of the employees of the company came from the Chinese partner, and some of them still felt more loyal to their old employer than to the foreign owners. Over time, these old loyalties were reinforced by the foreign partner's perceived lack of commitment: the overseas owners had appointed a single manager to oversee the factory and more senior representatives of the company traveled to China only intermittently, a couple of times a year. The overseas visitors came, complained, left, and waited for things to change. But things never did.

The foreign partner's involvement had obviously been too low from the beginning. Finally, there was no choice but to negotiate a sale of the JV to the Chinese partner. After months of discussions, the two sides parted amicably. The foreign partners received a fair payment for equipment and facilities that allowed them to recoup some of their losses.

The Chinese partner setting up a copycat operation is an extreme, if by no means unique, case. But getting control over how the company is run has proved to be one of the most intractable problems of JV's in general. Using an age-old Chinese adage, a joint venture has often been said to be two partners "sleeping in one bed but dreaming different dreams". Indeed, the whole rationale for entering into the relationship was often different for each party. The multinational partner would assume that the Chinese partner shared an ambition for building a strong company built on sound business principles, or at least that the ultimate goal was profit. Given that some local partners were politically managed state-owned enterprises with hazy business notions, this assumption was sometimes simply not true. Even when the local partner was a more market-savvy operation, local management ideally wanted the money and the technology and then to be left alone with running the company as it felt best. The foreign partner, on the other hand, would be looking for market access and for the opportunity to improve and streamline operations according to its worldwide experience of best practices. In some cases, local and overseas management would clash on everything from ethics and long-term business goals to operational and management issues. As a result, more time was spent on dealing and negotiating with the partner than actually dealing with the business and customers. In our opinion, there are ample reasons for not choosing the joint-venture format if it can be avoided — and for making sure that the legal framework is solid in those cases where a joint venture is necessary. A joint venture is somewhat akin to a franchise operation, where success is decided by the structuring of the legal entities involved.

So what do you do if you are forced to choose the JV format due to policy restrictions or find yourself managing a legacy JV? Fernandez and Underwood provide a useful discussion of how to select business partners by outlining a sequence of critical decisions you need to make, the first being: "Do you have a choice?". In this context, it is worth pointing out that some companies choose not to enter China at all because regulations would force them into an unwanted JV situation. In this sense, you always have a choice. But if you have decided to enter China knowing that it will have to include JV activities, there are still a number of decisions to make: How can the JV partner add value? Given that you need a partner, do you want him to be "weak", i.e. inactive and purely for regulatory reasons, or do you want a "strong" partner that will actually contribute to the business? How can you make sure that your goals are aligned as far as possible? And how can you manage the business relationship to build trust and foster effective decision making?

- *Take control*: If you find that things do not seem to be working out, try to take over the ownership by buying out the Chinese partner. In our experience, trying to "fix" a broken JV without full control will be difficult and time-consuming.
- *Align interests*: If you cannot obtain full ownership, then you must find a way of bringing the partner on board even if you

are the majority shareholder. Because even if you are, legacy and the fact that staff will come from the partner organization will give the partner a disproportional influence on day-to-day operations. Certain people in the JV organization can in practice only be influenced by the JV partner — because of old loyalties, personal guanxi, and the control over their future that this has often implied. You could say that in such cases, the local management will not quite get it when it comes to the concept of "ownership". Trying to implement change in this situation without having the partner on your side is doomed to fail.

- *Get rid of the problem*: If you cannot reach either of the above objectives, it is better to move out and cut your losses by selling or otherwise disposing of the business. Otherwise, you risk running yourself into a black hole of hopelessness. It will drain not only money, but more seriously also management resources and HQ patience.

Today, privately owned joint-venture partners will usually bring greater business acumen to the table, but this does not ensure that they will share your objectives. You may be wanting to crack the China market; they may be aiming to go abroad. You are looking for local business experience; they will be after your advanced production technology. Ideally, these wants and needs will complement each other, but in reality, mismatched expectations often lead to failure. We will deal with the general questions of finding Chinese business partners in the section that follows. But some particular things to think about when considering a joint venture in China are:

- *Do not be hasty*: China is a large country and you usually have more than one option. Too many foreign companies find partners in a passive or reactive fashion. If you are a large company, you may have been handed or appointed a partner by some central government authority. If you are a smaller company, you have often been approached by some prospective partner who would like to do business with you. In the former case, your options may be limited — but for a smaller company, China usually offers a wide range of partnership choices. Search the market for possible partners and start negotiations with the most suitable candidates.

- *Understand the decision-making structure*: Who is really calling the shots? This can be a fiendishly difficult question, and one that may come back to haunt you if it is not dealt with upfront. In a local state-owned enterprise, for example, the real power may lie with the Party secretary rather than the President or General Manager; if possible, you should also try to involve the relevant officials for the city or region in question. But the complex networks of informal guanxi of Chinese organizations can also introduce decision makers with influence way out of proportion to their formal titles. What is more, balances may change, sometimes rapidly, in the fast-moving Chinese environment.

- *Make sure agreements are realistic*: It is not uncommon for business partners to make promises that they cannot keep, whether because of lack of experience or simple wishful thinking; sometimes even because of pure desperation.

- *Make sure agreements are enforceable*: You may feel satisfied that you have ample contractual guarantees, even including penalties for breaches of agreement. But what if the partner simply has no money to pay? What if he has excellent guanxi with local utilities that can block production by cutting off energy or water? Local tax authorities? Banks? Courts? The written contract cannot necessarily provide protection — agreements in China must always be structured so that they make sense for both parties, and so that they punish both parties equally in the event of disagreement.

- *Beware of relatives*: In joint ventures, it is common for both parties to appoint not only Directors, but also to contribute senior management positions. It can be challenging to manage persons with strong connections, perhaps even family ties, to the joint-venture partner. This is a not a problem of the past — it keeps haunting business partnerships in China to this day.

6.3.3. *Wholly owned subsidiaries*

Nowadays, thanks to more liberal investment regulations, more and more foreign companies have started their own wholly owned companies in China without having a Chinese partner. These are officially called WFOEs (wholly foreign-owned enterprises). WFOEs are now the first choice for most foreign investors in China, the major advantages being the ability to manage the operations in a focused way without having to take into account the desires of a local partner. As a result of China's WTO entry, wholly owned companies have also received the right to import and export products, as well as to distribute products within China. In order to secure such trading rights, which were earlier limited to local Chinese companies, the company needs to amend or reapply for its business license.

6.3.4. *Acquisitions*

Over the last few years, financial deregulation has fostered an active M&A market in China. Most deals still involve international companies buying partial stakes in Chinese firms, but many companies now choose to establish wholly owned subsidiaries by acquiring local companies all-out.

Much of the experience from setting up and managing JV's still applies when you acquire a local company. For example, just as in the case of a JV, company employees may retain strong loyalties to the original owners or former colleagues, even though there are no longer any equity or other formal ties in place.

- *Try to buy the assets rather than the company*: Chinese companies often have hidden liabilities and other legacy issues. These risks can be reduced by purchasing the totality of assets: not just production facilities, buildings, inventory, and so on, but even accounts receivables and existing personnel structure. This approach makes all explicit.

- *Let the seller handle legacies*: For example, companies can suffer from overstaffing and bureaucracy. The selling party will often be in better position to handle such issues than you are; it is therefore usually better to let him solve perceived problems as a precondition of you acquiring the company.
- *Wait for the right opportunity*: Business cycles are beginning to affect China in the same way as other countries. This means that there will be times, when a company is cheaper to buy.

6.4. Finding and Managing Business Partner Relationships

A year or so ago, one of us worked with a Fortune-500 multi-national with extensive purchasing and sourcing operations in China. Like most multinationals, this company has a detailed "code of conduct" for suppliers which specifies that they must adhere to a number of ethical practices with respect to treatment of employees, environmental issues, and so on, in addition of course to obeying local laws and regulations.

The Chinese labor law has clear stipulations on maximum allowed overtime: no employee should be allowed to work for more than a stipulated number of hours per week. Enforcement of this law is lax, for several reasons. For employers, shorter work weeks raise costs. Factory workers often come from poor inland provinces and are eager to make as much money as possible during a limited number of years, in order to return home to get settle down and perhaps build a house with their accumulated savings. Local governments are eager to attract investments and so avoid challenging companies unless they are forced to.

(Continued)

(Continued)

Multinationals, however, are carefully monitored by consumer groups and governments in the countries they do business, and therefore need to enforce their code of conduct even in the face of this collusion between suppliers, supplier employees, and local government. Our client therefore monitors work hours to make sure that suppliers are not breaking the Chinese labor law.

On one inspection at a local textile manufacturer, our client was shown the punch cards of factory workers, which confirmed that they worked an average of 45 hours a week, with no employee working more than 46. But inspections at the quality department told a different story.

The quality department of every textile manufacturer is required to keep what is known in the industry as a "broken needle record". As garments are sewn, a needle will break from time to time. In order to avoid consumers being pricked in the armpit with the tip of a broken needle, the manufacturer will require that both parts of the needle be taped into a special record book before a new needle is provided to the seamstress. Each needle is time-stamped and the name of the seamstress written down.

Our client discovered that the incidence of broken needles was more or less the same day and night, seven days a week, and quickly calculated that this must mean that factory employees were working, on average, 70 hours a week. After three hours of obfuscation, where the supplier provided the wildest explanations for the inconsistency of the broken needle records with employee punch cards, he finally admitted to faking the working hours. It turned out that the supplier had a dedicated, full time employee whose job was to punch an "official" set of employee punch cards to show foreign customers. Factory employees were paid according to another set of (accurately stamped) punch cards.

It is not only in forming joint ventures that you will need business partners; you will need to form relationships with suppliers, distributors, and other local companies. Probably the single most prevalent cause of business failure in China is the wrong choice of partner, particularly in setting up joint venture or distribution deals.

In the case detailed above, the supplier was actually breaking Chinese law, but did not see anything wrong with that. "The workers want to work extra hours, because they are trying to save up for a house back home in their villages", the manager said, "the overseas customers demand the lowest prices, and the local government loves the tax revenue we generate. So why should I obey a law that nobody believes in?"

This attitude has its roots in the moral collapse of the Chinese political system, particularly during the so-called Cultural Revolution of the 1960s and 1970s. The planned economy made China into a society where getting ahead was usually at the expense of someone else. The results remain to this day: Tax discipline is low and a car ride through the traffic lights of any mid-sized Chinese city is ample proof that the legal system is only respected for as long as one is within eyesight of a representative of the law. More fundamentally, laws are flaunted since workers cannot form independent unions and therefore have a weak position against employers.

Problems with partners can take many forms besides failure to comply with stated codes of conducts. Fraser Mendel, the lawyer, lists a few typical scenarios that keep appearing in his practice:

- Suppliers pirate your products or produce extra quantities that are siphoned off for sales elsewhere, including for export.
- Suppliers produce products for your competitors despite non-competition clauses in your purchasing agreements.
- Distributors offer to register your trademarks in China, and with the signed affidavits in hand proceed to register these trademarks in their own name, something which may only be discovered years later.
- Suppliers may have impressive offices in a place like Hong Kong that do not reflect their actual operations in China. There have

even been cases where such storefront companies have solicited orders from Western customers and farmed these out to third-party vendors. When the customer was satisfied with the quality of the first shipment and placed a larger order, the supplier simply took off with the money.

- Some businesses in China are started to obtain finance, rather than obtaining finance to start a business. This is done by launching a basic production business, borrowing factory buildings, and renting equipment from the government with the collusion of friendly officials. The company then carries out low-level business for a period of time (e.g. a year) so as to establish a basic track record and persuade Western business partners to provide credit, for example in the form of advance payments for goods. Using the credit from the Western business partner as a seal of credibility, the company can then persuade a local bank to offer it loans. The management often repeats this process several times; when the Western partner and local bank have significant stakes in the company's survival, both can be persuaded to lend additional funds to overcome "short-term financial difficulties". When the financiers lose patience, the funds will have been siphoned off through related party transactions and the owner will have gone on a "business trip" abroad.

Clearly, in a market as complex and fast-moving as China's, partners can make or break your business. It is therefore important to find the right partners, and to protect yourself for potential contractual or other legal conflicts:

- *Look around*: Industries in China can be remarkably fragmented. At the beginning of the 21st century, there were still hundreds of independent auto manufacturers and dozens of refrigerator producers. When we did a survey of the market, we found that no company had more than 3% market share nationally in gas cookers and hobs. It pays to cast your net widely and to spend a lot of time comparing offers.

- *Look inside*: The sales office of your supplier may be nicely accessible, with pictures on the walls and a general professional feel to them. But you need to confirm that the supplier actually has the claimed staff and facilities as well as the necessary official documents showing their due incorporation, business license, possible industry-specific licenses, and qualifications. You also need to ascertain that the company has a serious track record of doing for-profit business.

- *Do not rely on intermediaries*: As we have mentioned above, one of the world's largest automotive manufacturers lost over a hundred million USD and several years in the market because they depended on the recommendations of a self-styled government relations consultant who claimed access to senior officials. Intermediaries and consultants can be an invaluable source of information, but you must be on top of the decision making. Do not allow anyone to dictate who you should partner with. There is always a second choice in China.

6.5. Due Diligence

Michael Ricks, who has rich experience from managing the four-billion dollar local business of a Fortune-500 multinational and later acquiring stakes in dozens of companies as a venture capitalist, provides some wonderful examples of why due diligence is so important in China: "The first thing to check is whether the company we are seeking to acquire has paid its taxes. We were buying a company in southern China and I put one of our juniors on doing the due diligence, pointing out that the company seemed to have unreasonably high profits, figures that I felt stood out because there was no scale or other leverage that would motivate these levels of returns. Unfortunately, it took our guy three months before he thought of checking if the company was paying its taxes. It turned out that they had not been paying a cent. Had we looked at this earlier, we could have saved a lot of time. Another case of failed due diligence was one of the major international banks pitching a private placement opportunity to us. When I looked at the prospectus, I immediately recognized one of the management team members: 'Wow, is this guy out of jail already', I asked the bank people, who were acutely embarrassed to learn that the person in question had siphoned off significant sums of money from his previous employer, a fact which had not surfaced during their investigation. Because of the lack of accessible registers, it is often difficult to find this kind of information during due diligence".

The situation is further exacerbated by the ready access to fake documents such as invoices and tax receipts. A 28 February 2008 article in The Economist describes an underground business that printed 1.05 trillion RMB worth of false tax receipts. The article finished by saying that "it is well known that Chinese companies often keep several sets of books. Yet the creation of entirely fictitious transactions, which can fool even the careful eyes of auditors and tax officials, suggests that investors need to be especially wary about where they put their money. Buyer — and tax man — beware".

Most companies in China, especially private ones, are of course run by honest, hardworking entrepreneurs. But due diligence does not just uncover malfeasance — it also exposes problems that may be due to systemic problems such as lax corporate governance or the endemic lack of qualified auditors and lawyers. Companies may have been restructured without good legal advice, and the sales team may be paying kickbacks to customers without the knowledge even of the company management. Doing your homework is therefore of paramount importance in any business dealing in China, be it a JV, a WFOE, an acquisition or a simple choice of business partner. Remember that you are in the Wild East! It is difficult to find background information on companies — even finding out if a potential partner has been properly incorporated can be a challenge. Spending money and resources upfront will save time and effort in the future. In setting up a local operation, there are several critical areas that are especially challenging:

- *Company ownership*: Partners can have complex ownership structures. This is true in the public sector — equity in what is usually referred to as "state-owned" enterprises can be held by government departments, provincial or municipal authorities, semi-independent associations or by other state-owned companies. Even the concept of "equity" is sometimes hazy: When Anders was discussing the acquisition of a major competing SOE in Hunan Province, he was orally presented with equity ownership figures that tallied to 120%. After some animated discussion, the ownerships of some of the parties were reduced in order to bring the total to 100%; this failed to immediately reassure Anders about the actual ownership situation.

Private companies, on the other hand, are often built around extended family relations and informal networks. Business deals often take the form of paperless handshakes: "I'll give you 5% of this subsidiary if you…". According to risk management consultant Peter Humphrey, some 70% of the private companies on which he does pre-acquisition due diligence for multinational clients display problems of this kind.

- *Company finances*: China's financial and auditing professions are only gradually catching up to worldwide standards. Because of corruption and lax enforcement from Chinese authorities, it is not uncommon for companies to keep more than one set of books: One for the taxman and one for management. Fraser Mendel, our lawyer friend, recalls a case where a manager was discovered to have kept four separate sets of accounts: "One set for the Chinese authorities and tax bureau; one set for the foreign shareholders; one set for the Chinese investors; and, since he himself was screwing foreign and Chinese owners alike, one for his own eyes only". It can be difficult to understand the financial situation even of a listed company in China and untangling the finances of a privately held company can be well-nigh impossible. The due diligence process must include secondary information and estimations of plausibility in addition to a careful scrutiny of the books. In the words of Peter Humphrey, "whichever set of books you look at, remember that it has been drafted for a purpose, with some specific reader in mind. It's not the numbers in an organization that matters, it's the people". Look for slush funds and unexplained cash payments that may indicate bribes to external parties. If you have to choose, hire a detective rather than an accountant to do your financial due diligence.

- *Liabilities*: It is common to discover problems with unpaid taxes, loans that have not been entered on the books and other undisclosed liabilities. The company may not have had the cash to make tax payments, in which case local tax authorities may be lying in wait for new investors to come in, pouncing on the opportunity to collect outstanding debts. This can be a problem for any investor, but foreign companies are known to be easier targets and often seen to have deeper pockets than local players. Other potential liabilities are unpaid duties for imported goods and unpaid pensions for workers.

- *Sales figures*: In evaluating a company, the sales pipeline is a key factor. It is not uncommon to come across companies where recent sales figures have been inflated through phantom contracts — in the words of Mike Ricks, "someone calls his industry buddies at the end of the quarter and signs a bunch of large orders that are promptly canceled at the beginning of the next quarter". Of course, in any market you will see some degree of manipulation of sales figures — deferred or prepaid contracts in order to smooth out the sales curves, for example. Here, it is a matter of degree. More commonly, the sales organization will have been paying bribes and kickbacks to customers. This will probably be untenable for your own organization once you acquire the company, and can result in loss of existing customers for the company after the acquisition. It is advisable to use circumspect methods to get a feel for the sales pipeline. For a consumer goods company, this might, for example, entail talking to shop attendants to see if products are really selling out of shops, not just going in as inventory.

- *Ownership of assets*: The complex ownership structures outlined above apply equally to a particular company's rights to its claimed assets. But an equally serious potential problem is the stripping of state-owned assets that have taken place over the last few years in China — some of the large private companies in China, particularly industrial companies, were started in this way. The leadership of a state-owned company can strip assets by selling them off to a newly formed venture at fire-sale prices. According to Peter Humphrey, large multinationals have encountered serious issues as such legacies from previous acquisitions have come to the surface.

- *Land use rights*: A particularly salient example of asset ownership is land use rights. In China all land is owned by the state. It is only the right to use the land that can be purchased. Buying land use rights in a development zone to build one's own factory is normally not too complicated or risky, but when you are taking over an existing company, you need to establish that land use rights are unequivocal and undisputed, and that there are no purchase costs or registration fees outstanding from the company. It is not uncommon for land use rights to be owned by another company or cooperative than the prospective acquisition target or joint-venture partner, even though it appears on the balance sheet of the company. You also need to make sure that the land is actually possible to use in the way you intend. We have already cited the example of the foreign company which acquired a factory with land use rights, only to discover that the access railway cut straight through a military installation and was therefore off limits to the foreign company in transporting its goods.
- *IPR*: It is not uncommon for companies to have been built around stolen or disputed technologies or patents. Due diligence should include the ownership of all IPR.
- *Environment*: Before signing a contract to buy a company or to form a joint venture, a careful study must be made of the impact the present company might have had on its environment. China has its own "Love Canals" — over the years, local companies have disposed of dangerous substances by digging them down instead of the more costly way of letting a destruction company handle them. A ground study is a must.

These problems do not always have direct or immediate consequences — but they certainly create sleepless nights for management and undermine headquarter confidence in the China operations. "In any case", says Peter Humphrey, "such legacy issues can create uncomfortable leverage from business partners or individuals in the know, leverage that can influence your China operations for a long time to come".

6.6. Consultants

At one time or another, every company will need to resort to the services of consultants — be they lawyers, accountants, or marketing professionals. But the quality of consultants in China varies enormously. The main reason for this is fast growth: There is a huge dearth of professionals. An *Economist* article from 11 January 2007 makes the point for the accounting profession: "By even the most generous reckoning, [China] has fewer than 70,000 practicing accountants, trying to do the work of anything from 300,000 to a million bean counters". It is unusual to find professionals with more than 10 years of industry experience: "To be an accounting student at a reputable school is to have a good job waiting. But even after several years of education, accountants require an apprenticeship, especially if they are to get to grips with international standards based on intellectually demanding principles rather than prescriptive rules". The same thing could be said for most of the professions.

The Economist also outlines the legacy reasons for the lack of professional standards. Under the state economic system, education focused on aspects of the profession that are simply not relevant to a modern market economy: "Businesses reported information that would interest a centrally planned economy, such as production quotas. The measuring sticks of bourgeois managers — costs, debt, depreciation, and (of course) profit — were ignored." This has left older accountants woefully unprepared for the requirements of the 21st century.

Multinational consulting firms have a large presence in China, but they often suffer from a lack of understanding of local conditions. Mike Ricks points out that "you don't want the guy who just

got off the plane from New York — there are lots of highly qualified foreign professionals who are relocated to China to meet the
fast local growth of their firm, but who lack the relevant local experience to provide any meaningful advice whatsoever". In some
areas, such as law, international firms are restricted from providing
direct services and must work through local partners.

The lack of experienced consultants has serious ramifications:
Do not expect proactive, senior advice — in most instances, the
client will need to manage the consultancy more closely than in
developed markets. In creative industries such as advertising and
PR, finding agencies that can be original and think outside the box
is a real challenge.

The explosive growth of the Chinese economy also means that
mediocre or outright unprofessional service providers survive that
would have been quickly weeded out in more mature markets.
Some of these will be mom-and-pop shops which depend on personal relationships with a single client for their existence; for
example, there are more than 1,000 registered PR firms in Beijing
alone! Recruitment firms, which have proliferated wildly in one of
the most overheated industries in China, are notorious: Expect the
quality of candidates to fluctuate widely and do not assume that
the headhunter has performed more than perfunctory background
checks. In some disciplines, you will be served by rookies who may
lack even the basic competencies needed to provide professional
services.

When choosing consultants for your China venture, here are
some of the things to look for:

- *Local experience*: Credentials often look impressive, but need to
  be carefully scrutinized. Local firms will frequently list nonexistent clients and spurious case studies. Multinational firms
  will cite cases from abroad to flesh out their local credentials.
- *People*: Who are the consultants that will actually be serving
  your account? Consultancies will tend to bring in GM and
  Director-level people for the "pitch", but these are certainly not
  the professionals who will be dealing with your organization

on a day-to-day basis. In buying consulting services, you should be shopping for the services of particular individuals rather than their company. Make sure you have had the chance to meet the people you will actually be working with. Check the impressive CV's of the expatriate consultants: how long have they been in China, and what have they really done that is relevant to the local market?

- *The local/international mix*: It is about bridging the culture gap. Otherwise, you risk getting either technically competent people without the necessary cultural skills to relate to you and your business, or local juniors who lack international-level technical skills.

But of course, the factor which will really decide your success in China is not which consultants you choose, but how you find, hire, develop, and retain a winning local team of colleagues. This is the topic of our next chapter.

Chapter 7

A Winning Local Team

In our opinion, the ability to identify, recruit, develop, and retain local talent is *the* key to success in China. At the same time, how best to develop the human resources of one's China organization remains one of the most contentious issues among expatriate and local managers alike.

In the 1990s, the perceived lack of loyalty of Chinese staff was widely discussed in expatriate management circles. Senior Chinese coworkers were said to happily change jobs for no more than a small salary increase, regardless of other factors. "Chinese people just work for the money — if somebody offers them a 1,000 RMB raise, they will leave immediately". "It doesn't pay to invest in employees in China, because as soon as you have trained them, they will join a competitor". These are authentic, and oft-repeated statements from informal discussions between Western managers in China.

Anders' experience was different. It quickly became obvious that, without paying excessive salaries, Sandvik still had low staff turnover. Salaries are important everywhere, including China, but Chinese employees actually seemed to respond positively to the same things as people do in the West. Our observations ranged from obvious things like interesting and well-defined tasks which are challenging but within one's ability to complete successfully, training and career possibilities, to soft values like participation in decision making and the perception of working for a successful company.

Anders got the nicest possible receipt one day on loyalty, when he heard one of his young local salesmen walking over to his secretary and saying something in an angry voice. A loud discussion took place. They were both truly upset. When Anders asked, they decided to tell him what the discussion was about. The young man had been approached by a headhunter, who wanted him to change jobs and go to work for another company.

At the time, headhunting was still a rather new phenomenon. The young sales rep was simply upset that somebody would be calling him to offer another position. Anders secretary shared his sentiments and the two of them handed Anders the headhunter's phone number, more or less demanding that he should phone the company and tell them to stop encouraging our people to leave. Anders did so and the (very surprised) foreign manager of the headhunting company stuttered that she was only doing her job, but that of course they would stop calling and offering jobs to people working for us. Hearing this telephone conversation, our two people were satisfied.

7.1. A Human Resource-Scarce Environment

7.1.1. *Theory X or theory Y?*

In his book "The Human Side of Enterprise" from 1960, Douglas McGregor of Harvard proposed two theories of human behavior in the workplace: theories X and Y. Theory X was classic command-and-control management "reflecting an underlying belief that management must counteract an inherent human tendency to avoid work". Theory Y, by contrast, "assumes that people will exercise self-direction and self-control in the achievement of organizational objectives to the degree that they are committed to those objectives". A review of the modern workplace in *The Economist* puts it like this: "theory X is bent on devising the right sticks with which to prod work-shy labor; theory Y looks for the carrots that will induce them to stay".

Of course, theories X and Y have roots in more fundamental questions explored by ancient philosophers, in the West as well as in China. A couple of thousand years before McGregor, Chinese thinkers contemplated whether man was intrinsically good or evil. Confucius' disciple Mencius claimed that people are basically "good" — in other words, he was a proponent of theory Y. Unfortunately for modern Chinese workers, local companies can still be strong proponents of theory X. But it also seems that, as a result of this influence or perhaps a more general suspicion of local employees, Western managers are more prone to believe in theory X in China than they would be in their home countries.

Chinese economic realities present compelling arguments for embracing theory Y. This is because a rapidly growing economy such as China's creates a market which is scarce in experienced human resources. Take Johan's industry of Public Relations as an example. Starting in the 1990s, the Chinese PR industry has grown by 30% per year. If we assume, for the sake of argument, that the industry 10 years ago consisted of 100 PR consultants, who had just entered the profession, this industry growth would mean that 10 years later, about 1,060 consultants would be needed.

If we continue to consider that, because of the overall growth of the Chinese economy, some 10% of consultants leave agencies and move to the client side (a low estimate, considering that China's economy has grown by about 10% per year, and foreign-invested enterprises have multiplied even more rapidly). Let us also assume that another 10% move on to different careers, to study abroad, and so on, the original 100 consultants would by now have been reduced to just 13 people.

In other words, we would have only 13 consultants with 10 years of experience remaining in agencies to manage some 1,060 fresh recruits, a ratio approaching 1:100.

Graph 1: Number of consultants needed assuming 30% industry growth.

Year	Consultants
1	100
2	130
3	169
4	220
5	286
6	371
7	483
8	627
9	816
10	1060

Graph 2: Number of original consultants remaining in agencies after 10 years, assuming 10% annual attrition due to overall market growth and 10% due to career changes.

Year	Consultants
1	100
2	80
3	64
4	51
5	41
6	33
7	26
8	21
9	17
10	13

We have already seen how this situation affects the availability of qualified professionals in law, accounting, PR, and consulting. But the shortage of experienced professionals affects enterprises just as profoundly. There are several reasons for the lack of management talent:

- China's recent history: The modern management profession is a relative novelty in China. During the Cultural Revolution schools and universities closed so that lack of academic qualifications prevented a whole generation from maturing into potential corporate leaders.

- The hypercompetitive local environment: As we have seen, in most industries in China, all major multinationals will be present, and in turn collectively competing against scores of local companies. This does not just apply to market share — you are also competing for the best employees. And while multinationals still enjoy an advantage in attracting Chinese recruits, the local competitors are also gradually waking up to the importance of competitive human resource strategies. The real battle for talent has not even started yet in China.

- Fast market growth: When the economy as a whole is growing at 10%, and the hottest industries much faster than that, there simply are not enough people to go around. The talent pool may be expanding as Chinese universities churn out ever increasing numbers of graduates, but the proportion of experienced recruits will, by definition, be smaller than in a market with slower growth. This also means that you are likely to lose valuable colleagues to other fields of business than your own — experienced managers are so valuable that they are often recruited across industries.

This has profound implications for managers. In an environment like this, sales — finding more clients — will not be the main bottleneck for growth. Recruitment, development, and retention will be. In essence, your company will be competing with other companies for the best recruits. By recruiting the best, developing them and enticing them to stay, you will have an unassailable competitive advantage on the Chinese market. This becomes especially important in the service sector, where "the employee is the product". It is also critical in sales organizations, where customers may be more loyal to a particular sales person than to the supplying company and its product. In such cases, the company may lose both employee and customer when somebody leaves.

Another consequence of working in a resource-scarce environment is that you will usually need to deal with younger people. A more mature organization in Europe or the US usually has a fair number of older employees, but in China, the average age at a multinational may well be around 30! Young people will, of course, often be ambitious, energetic, and eager to learn. But at the same time they sometimes lack the people skills and management experience that can only come from maturity. Whereas skilled workers and technicians are easy to find, "lack of experienced managers" regularly tops Chamber of Commerce surveys as the greatest human resource challenge in China.

The only way to solve this problem is to hire for potential and develop your own talent. Paradoxically, it can be easier to retain high-fliers than mediocre employees. High-fliers will receive well-deserved promotions and salary raises, but more ordinary coworkers will compare their own moderate raises to friends and colleagues and become restless if they come out at the bottom of this comparison.

7.1.2. *Chinese employees can be just as loyal as any others*

Based on our experience, Chinese employees are loyal to their employer — if the employer treats them fairly. In China — as in most other countries — employees will usually leave because of their relationship with an individual manager rather than salary or other aspects of the company itself. This phenomenon is actually especially pronounced in China, since employees tend to be more relation orientated than in the West. The high turnover of staff at multinational companies is, like so many business problems in China, the result of failure to understand the psychology of local people combined with a lack of consistent management practices.

China is a country in rapid change. With incessant change, people learned that the only people they could trust were family and the closest circle of friends.

The current legal and business environment strengthens the feeling among employees that it's a dog eat dog world in China. Enterprises sometimes disregard existing laws and regulations. In 2005, the Ministry of Labor published figures indicating that many companies did not provide workers with written contracts, despite clear stipulations in the national labor law requiring them to do so. In 2008, a new labor law was promulgated that give employees stronger rights against employers, and provides tougher punishments for companies that do not adhere to regulations, but getting 100% compliance from firms will take time.

Western companies often have strict worldwide codes of conduct that require them to obey rules and regulations. They are monitored by international NGO's, and are even held to higher standards than Chinese enterprises by local authorities — they are expected to pay taxes and to follow rules and regulations to the letter. Breaches of laws and regulations, especially those that are costly to implement such as environmental regulations, by local companies are therefore frequent points of contention for foreign business people and politicians who feel they create an unfair playing field.

Against this background, Chinese recruits join a foreign-invested enterprise with high expectations. They expect a multinational to be fair, transparent, follow the law, be managed "by rules" rather than "by individuals", and providing a safe work environment — precisely because they sometimes fail to find these virtues in local companies. Chinese employees are deeply skeptical of "rule by person" and tend to demand clear regulations in every area of activity — later, we will look at a specific example: the need for transparency in salary systems. More generally, one could say employees are probably vigilant about anything seen as favoritism simply because they are so used to and fed up with it. And because of this, they expect foreign managers to curb rule by person in the organization as a whole.

Providing a feeling of security to employees is also important. Chinese citizens used to depend on their "danwei", the work unit, to provide their social security. The danwei catered for workers from cradle to grave in what was known as "the iron rice bowl"; kindergarten, healthcare and sickness benefits, housing and pensions were all taken care of by the work unit. If you wanted to get married, you had to get the signature of your boss. You were guaranteed employment until the pension age of 50 (for women) or 55 (for men). For state employees, it was socialist paradise.

During the 1990's, the safety net based around the danwei social security system finally came apart. The government has tried to set up alternative health and retirement insurance, but the general consensus is that these reforms have so far failed to provide a robust system; in the wake of the international financial crisis of 2008 and 2009, the authorities are making a more concerted attempt at welfare reform. Psychologically, Chinese employees still generally calculate with having to care for themselves.

Companies also exacerbate the trust and security concerns of employees by acting short term. Multinationals tend to send in expatriate managers that spend short stints of three or fewer years at the local subsidiary. These managers, who have no particular interest in China other than as a springboard on the multinational career ladder, will be concerned primarily with showing a good, or improving, bottom line during their short tenure with the local organization.

Put yourself in the shoes of the bright and ambitious young Chinese career person who enters a multinational company. The trust deficit, and the overall suspicion of "rule by person" means frequent management changes at the top will be seen as a lack of commitment. If the manager, preoccupied with the bottom line, does not show clear investments in developing the human resources of the company, this will further compound this impression. In the end, the local employee will ask herself: "why should I commit to a company that clearly is not committing to me?" In such a mindset, when the unavoidable call from the headhunter comes, the person will certainly try to pursue a higher salary.

In Western Europe, and to a lesser extent in the US, "work-life balance" has long been an important topic for the majority of white-collar workers. But in China, this is simply not the case.

At Eastwei, we have come to accept that people will choose to work 12-hour days even though we have done our best to promote more sustainable work habits — even when we do not pay for the overtime and have removed opportunities to convert vacation days to cash, people tend to stay at the office voluntarily.

Chinese people sometimes relate to their company in a more direct way than Westerners. Joining an organization is like marrying into a family — it requires a mutual commitment from both parties. In our experience, Chinese employees are at least as loyal, probably more, as those of most other countries — if you show that you care about them as persons and are willing to invest in seeing them grow with your company. Our subjective feeling is borne out by research by human resource consultancy Watson Wyatt on the Chinese market. Whereas money is one key motivator, education and personal betterment are much stronger. If you want to lower staff turnover and increase loyalty, here are some of the things to do:

- *Show management commitment*: Try to find managers that can build rapport with local colleagues and who are willing to stay for at least four years in China.
- *Show that you care*: Reinforce the sense of belonging and the "family feeling" of the company. There are many little ways of doing this: If one of your direct reports is ill for more than a day or two, senior management sending flowers or, better yet, visiting with a fruit basket or other gift, will be seen as a strong signal of care.
- *Invest in your people*: Show that you are committed to their growth, with "no strings attached". The best way to kill loyalty is to ask employees to sign formal documents where they "guarantee" that they will continue to work for the company for a certain period of time, or pay back training costs if they leave prematurely. And anyway, it will not keep them from leaving if they feel they are not growing in their present position.
- *Keep holding out future enticements*: Not asking employees to sign formal contracts in return for training does not mean you

have to give up the carrot of development opportunities. A foreign company has unique possibilities to actively foster loyalty by sending employees abroad for training and study tours. To go to a foreign country as part of one's work is still an important event for a local employee. By setting a long-term schedule for overseas training, you make sure the local colleague constantly has something to look forward to.

- *Engage families*: Chinese children will often live at home until they get married, and sometimes beyond that time. Chances are that your 30-something employees will still be living with their parents. They also care a great deal about what parents, spouses, and other relatives think about their jobs and careers. You should therefore take every opportunity to engage families. Formal arrangements can include an office open house for families, an annual family dinner, or simply making sure that colleagues abroad send Christmas cards — these will often be placed in a prominent place at home for family and friends to look at and can contribute to loyalty. In general, allowing colleagues to look important in front of their families will reinforce their own positive feelings about the company. This can create a strong bond.

So, who are these young, ambitious white-collar workers that will make or break your success in China? Let us have a more detailed look at some of the key traits and how they impact management practices.

7.2. Characteristics of the Chinese Workforce

We have already explored some of the environmental factors that have shaped Chinese coworkers. Let us now look at some of the general characteristics of the Chinese workforce, and some of the other factors that influence Chinese colleagues. Although they are of course generalizations, these observations are based on our own experience as well as discussions with many of our peers at other companies.

7.2.1. *Chinese coworkers are young, well educated, and ambitious*

A Japanese business acquaintance of ours once remarked that "Westerners see Japan as competitive, but China today is a way more cut-throat society than Japan is". Indeed, in the eyes of most expatriate managers, Chinese coworkers are intensely aggressive and therefore tend to be impatient and want quick results. There are many reasons for this. One is simply that there are so many people in China trying to get ahead; this is further exacerbated by an education system which continuously ranks children in each subject.

There are also so many choices open to young Chinese as the economy develops. Young people can pick and choose. Mr. Kawasaki, a 25-year Sony veteran who has spent seven years in China, noted that "in Europe and Japan, employees are motivated by becoming more and more distinguished experts in some specialization — in China, people want to be promoted, to be managers, to have titles and to rapidly increase salaries". One way of achieving this is by increasing the number of levels, which allows for "mini-promotions" where the first step may entail having responsibility for a working group of only two or three people.

People below 30 are the most difficult to keep. Older colleagues start understanding the career plan, opportunities for growth, and the path to senior positions. Turnover in the above 30 age group is therefore often lower. The higher volatility among fresh university graduates is a strong argument for hiring young people with at least a couple of years of work experience. Chinese university studies are theoretically focused and campus life shelters students from the realities of working life and society as a whole. Young people mature quickly after only a year or two of professional life; this makes them more valuable for employers. It also allows them to attain a clearer career direction and makes them less prone to jump ship in the short term.

As we have seen, Chinese coworkers tend to be young and ambitious. But the typical employee is also well educated — it is quite common at all multinationals in China to find university degrees in jobs where in the West this would more seldom be the case, for example secretarial and junior sales positions.

The prevalence of over-qualification in China means one has to devise internal promotion paths for individuals in many positions in order to avoid losing these people to competitors. This can be done to mutual benefit.

Both of us have had secretaries and other support staff with excellent academic backgrounds in engineering, business, etc. One such person sought a secretarial position from within the company after having worked as Inside Sales in one of our product divisions, because she saw the job as the Executive Secretary for the company President as a position in which she could learn more and develop better. The transition went well. She did an excellent job, but it quickly became obvious that she would not stay in this position for the rest of her life. Being gifted and ambitious, she took advantage of the company's scheme to pay for "relevant education" done in the employee's free time. She entered an MBA course at Peking University and completed her degree with the highest scores among her 100 fellow students. She had chosen an MBA with an HR profile. By investing in her personal development, we were able to keep this qualified employee for seven years. Johan actively uses the receptionist and secretarial positions as a way of offering employment to fresh university graduates, who can then be moved to junior consulting trainee positions after they have accumulated one or two years of working experience.

The work-life balance is, as we have mentioned elsewhere, heavily skewed in favor of the workplace. Success is what counts. Chinese employees are impatient; they will typically emphasize personal development as the most important short-term job satisfaction factor and will not hang around for long if they do not feel they are advancing or bettering themselves. Long vacations and flexible hours are typically not particularly attractive to recruits, who would much rather get a higher salary or faster advancement.

7.2.2. *Many successful managers are women*

Women in China are emancipated and make up half the workforce. So does sex matter when you choose professionals and managers in China? Some Western managers, perhaps influenced by stereotypes of the Orient in general, tend to worry that women may be excluded from certain areas of business in China and will thus prefer hiring male staff. In our experience, the opposite may be just as true.

General considerations of corporate ethics and equal opportunity policies aside, there are strong reasons for hiring for talent rather than sex in China. Far from being discriminated against in the workplace, Chinese women tend to be well represented in most professions. Chinese women are often career focused, and the one-child policy means most women continue working with only a short interruption for childbirth. Helpful parents or in-laws and the availability of inexpensive domestic help are other factors that make it easier for working women to be successful in the workplace even as they raise a family. Chinese universities now enroll a higher percentage of women than of men.

Women also make up a much higher proportion of the promoted staff than in any other country where we have worked. Talking to the manager of a large Japanese company, we asked him what he thought of female managers. "It's almost like I don't dare to tell you", he said, "people might think I have this thing for women. But to tell you the truth, we don't have a single man in the senior middle management of our company in China. Why? Because the women beat their male counterparts in almost every aspect of management: they work harder (which is the same in Japan), they are more flexible and open to change, they speak better English, and they are way ahead in soft management skills".

Indeed, this may be an Asian phenomenon rather than a purely Chinese one. Chris Lee, who has headed several multinational healthcare companies in Asia, including China, and now manages the Asia-Pacific region for Bayer Schering Pharmaceuticals, once told us the story of how he built a greenfield operation for a multi-national in Korea: "People told me I could only hire male sales representatives because, supposedly, they had to entertain the customers in karaoke bars and massage parlors. I thought that was a narrow minded way of thinking and decided to do the exact opposite: hire women exclusively. The result? They worked harder than the men, were more loyal to the company and were also more open to international management practices than their male peers. Plus I saved a fortune in entertainment costs!"

In managerial positions, several of the managers and Human Resource consultants we have talked to assert that women tend to be less ego conscious and more flexible than their male counterparts. Women are seen as less traditional — more open, more adaptable, and more progressive — than their male counterparts. Be such generalizations as they may — it is clear that Chinese women are a resource and should in no way be discriminated against during the recruitment or promotion process. Conversely, we have in discussions with female foreign managers heard of no obstacles that hinder the success of Western business women in leading positions in China.

7.2.3. *Age and education count in the reporting structure*

Even though Chinese women are successful in the modern workforce, it still happens from time to time that men feel uncomfortable being managed by women. But seniority is a more important problem in this context. Confucian tradition places great emphasis on respect for elders, and it is therefore often difficult for young managers to garner the authority and self-confidence to manage older colleagues. Conversely, older employees will balk at being told what to do by someone younger than themselves.

Although sex and age can play havoc with management structures, the most troublesome area is the reluctance to be managed by someone with a lower education than oneself. This is due to the excessive emphasis placed on traditional education and formal diplomas and certificates in China.

7.2.4. *Formal education carries great weight*

For at least 2000 years, since the Han dynasty, China was administered by a ruling class of "mandarins", steeped since early childhood in the tenets of Confucianism, a worldview which emphasizes a harmonious society based on relationships between ruler and ruled, parent and child, older brother and younger brother, husband and wife, and between friends. To become a member of the imperial administration, a child was trained to memorize the Confucian classics and was then tested in a series of examinations culminating in the palace exams held in Beijing's Forbidden City.

This emphasis on Confucian learning has had a profound influence on Chinese society to this day, both because of the social values inculcated by Confucianism itself, but also because the imperial examination system made China into a meritocracy, unlike Europe which was a hereditary "feudal" society until the advent of democracy in the last century or two. The road to success in ancient China has always been studies. As in most Asian societies, the respect for formal education is therefore great. Modern Chinese families will spend a large proportion of their resources to ensure that children are educated in the best way possible.

Employees will actively pursue MBA programs and other adult education in parallel to a demanding career. On-the-job training is seen as a major motivating factor.

The downside of the preoccupation with education and formal degrees is that it is sometimes hard for educated people to accept leadership from people with a lower academic background, no matter how practically experienced the latter may be. Expatriates are often seen as "different" enough that this does not become a major issue. But we have seen several cases where having a lower level of education than the local employees has become a problem for managers from Hong Kong and Taiwan.

7.2.5. *Chinese coworkers are individualistic*

Contrary to common Western perceptions, Chinese people in general are quite individualistic. From a young age, they are trained as individuals; where Westerners play football and do group study projects, Chinese students are taught to be intensely competitive at the individual level. Students are continuously ranked in each subject — you can immediately see who in each class is doing "better" and "worse" than yourself. This kind of ranking, which is particularly common in younger employees, leads Chinese employees to see success as a zero-sum game.

The somewhat myopic focus on the relative success of others brings different management challenges as well. In Sweden and England, Anders had always announced internal positions as a way of showing employees that internal recruitment would create opportunities for everyone. In China, he stopped because for every happy successful candidate he would create four extremely unhappy ones, who felt that not being appointed was a huge "loss of face". In fact, applicants in China sometimes tell all their friends and family members both that they have applied and that they are sure of getting the job. This does not tend to make the issue of face loss any easier, should they in fact not get the offer.

The lack of early exposure to teamwork means it is more difficult to automatically expect good results from teams in China than in any other place we have worked. If you assign a team or task force to a specific assignment in the West, you can often leave the team to it. In China, you need to be heavily involved, even if you assign a clear team leader. Otherwise, more often than not, nothing happens. One reason is that it tends to be difficult for the team leader to get authority unless the team is a long-standing grouping with formal positions. Both of us have, however, relied heavily on the work of teams and task forces as an important method of developing employees and preparing them for managerial roles.

Another challenge stemming from an individualistic, zero-sum mindset is that Chinese colleagues tend to be reluctant to share information. In the words of Jöerg Wuttke, Chief Representative of German chemicals giant BASF, they are "'information black holes' — whatever goes in never comes out again, people don't share with their colleagues".

7.2.6. *Few people will voluntarily stick their neck out*

Besides the lack of training in teamwork, one of the most hotly debated consequences of the Chinese educational system is the lack of critical thinking. Although younger people are more critical and tend to speak their mind more, it is still a major problem, which is reinforced by the general unwillingness to express a different opinion — tradition, education, and politics have all conspired to punish Chinese people for sticking their necks out. An *Economist* article on 6 October 2006 entitled "The battle for brains" discusses China in the context of a more general global talent shortage: "China's biggest problem is a culture of deference — a culture that was refined by the mandarin tradition... for many Chinese it is seen as provocative, even obnoxious, to question superiors."

This tendency to be conservative and overcautious is further exacerbated by the preoccupation with what others think about you. People want to be well liked and often go to great lengths to avoid open conflict. This behavior is deeply ingrained in the local psyche; people generally tend to be relationship oriented and enormously considerate towards friends and family. But at its worst, it can seriously influence results; as a colleague at a large multinational remarked, "in China, you have to be vigilant about people who don't add value, just shuffle work from point A to point B without really contributing to the result".

A Western manager does not expect people to simply agree if they have a different opinion. We want, even expect, that opinion on the table where it can be openly discussed. It takes a long time and a lot of friendly coaching to make a local Chinese employee comfortable with the fact that we want management ideas discussed and scrutinized.

Changing the conformist mindset is of course more important in some industries and positions than in others. In consulting, the ability to foster a creative climate of debate and questioning of the status quo is one of the keys to excellent client service. In order to encourage internal questioning and debate, Johan actually staged pre-arranged debates during the company's Monday meetings — senior consultants were asked to criticize management decisions at the meetings so that the juniors would get used to a straight-forward and open discussion climate. During the first few meetings, the juniors would look nervously at each other: "are these guys crazy to talk to the boss like that?" But after a couple of weeks of continuing debates without anyone getting fired, the juniors started throwing themselves into the fray with great relish.

This active fostering of desired cultural traits in the organization has more general applications. New coworkers, for example, often need to be ushered into the community — otherwise, they tend to sit there alone when everyone else leaves for lunch. The cure may be as simple as just asking one of the people who usually go to lunch to bring the new colleague along. There seems to be no deliberate distancing taking place in cases like these — just a lack of compassion for the new person. Just as people in China are usually exceedingly thoughtful when it comes to friends and relatives, there seems to be a general lack of consideration for people outside this immediate circle. People will push and shove, park their cars in the middle of the road or their bicycles on the pavement, rather than leaving space for others. If you want the team to be consider-ate to each other, you may need to actively promote such behavior.

Another way of encouraging coworkers to contribute their opinions is simply learning how to listen to them without volun-teering your own ideas. Your local colleagues will often be at a language disadvantage in addition to the cultural predisposition to passively listening to the boss. We often hear Western managers pontificate endlessly to their captive Chinese management team. In the words of Jöerg Wuttke of BASF, "the notion of waiting, the tor-ture of silence, can be difficult for expatriate managers — but if you manage to keep silent, it is much easier to encourage your local people to speak". We have also found that employees sometimes need to be directly prompted, schoolteacher-style, to speak out in larger meetings.

When junior colleagues try to sound you out by asking for your opinion on an issue, make it a habit never to express your own thoughts without first having replied with a "what do you think"? This method of forcing out suggestions works well short term, and even better over the long term — after a while, people realize that they are not getting useful guidance, so they stop asking and start taking responsibility.

For a manager, group-think can become especially serious when it comes to evaluating fellow employees. At one of Anders's companies, we had a local office IT engineer who became viewed as a serious problem. At the outset, he seemed a bit "different" or odd, somewhat outside the rest of the organization. Gradually, talk inside our organization became so critical, saying that he lacked qualifications, bought the wrong equipment and did not work hard enough, that everyone, including management, accepted the problems at face value. Things got so serious that the rumors reached the head office IT function, and Anders received an order to "do something about the problem". But as Anders and his senior IT manager investigated the case, they found that the engineer was doing a great job, and was at least as qualified as most of the other engineers. None of the original complaints could be substantiated, and it became obvious that the poor guy had been caught in an increasingly vicious cycle of rumors. Both of us have seen similar cases in our own and other local organizations.

7.2.7. *Coworkers are technically proficient but lack "soft" skills*

Another side effect of the emphasis on theory combined with the individualistic bent of Chinese coworkers is the shortage of soft skills — particularly in management and communications — and a failure to see the "big picture". The tendency of local colleagues to adhere to "what they have been told to do" rather than anticipating the desired results and working proactively to achieve them can be intensely frustrating for expatriate managers. Mr. Kawasaki, a SONY veteran of 25 years who has spent seven years in China and six in the Middle East, put it succinctly: "This is the biggest difference between China and other markets where I have worked. People understand sales, but not marketing; they know accounting but not finance; they do delivery but don't understand logistics; they install 'computers' rather than 'management information systems'. The key challenge in China is to guide and educate our colleagues in seeing this bigger business perspective".

Jöerg Wuttke of BASF pointed out the serious business consequences of lacking critical thinking for business intelligence and investment intelligence: "People just look at our own plans without seeing the strategic business challenges, for example, what will our competitors be doing? People just extrapolate current growth tends for our own company without considering what would happen if CIBA sets up the same facilities as ours in Shanghai?"

Part of the problem also stems from the youth of Chinese colleagues. Wuttke continues: "Here, the longest-standing employee is our driver who has been with us for 15 years. Then there are two GM's with 12 years in the company. You have German expatriates with 20 years of industry experience being replaced with locals of five years experience. So it is sometimes not fair to expect the same big-picture thinking from these younger employees".

7.2.8. *Language is a limiting factor*

We have already stressed the importance of having access to excellent translation and interpretation. Foreign managers who speak good Chinese are still in the minority, so English-speaking local recruits are in high demand. But language skills are in short supply and will remain so for a long time to come. This means that, oftentimes, you have to balance language skills against other salient criteria in recruiting coworkers. Remember that language skills can be acquired, while basic character traits and attitude cannot. Still, finding the balance between language ability and other job-related skills and qualities can be tricky.

When speaking in English to a colleague, you must always be aware of the risk that, while nodding vigorously and otherwise indicating acquiescence in every way, he or she has not, in fact, understood what is being said. Not understanding can be seen as a loss of face.

7.2.9. *Employees will avoid overtly challenging managers*

Confucianism emphasizes deep respect for, and total submission to, authority. In "the five relationships", Confucius summarized the interactions between lord and subject, parent and child, husband and wife, older brother and younger brother, and between friend and friend. In all but the last one, deference must be absolute. On the other hand, the superior party in each relationship has a moral imperative to be "good" to the lesser one.

Respect for authority and an unwillingness to stick one's neck out conspire to form one of the most frustrating and intractable challenges for expatriate managers in China: low-level procrastination as a way of opposing unpopular decisions or policies. You "agree" with the boss — but then "forget" to act on this agreement. This can be aggravating to a Western manager, who expects coworkers to speak their minds about a decision, but then implement it to the letter once it has been made. In China, this issue is all-pervasive — it will come up in any discussion on management. There are basically three ways of dealing with it:

- *Engagement and ownership*: the only real solution to the low-level procrastination problem is to ensure that coworkers have truly bought into projects and tasks. We will discuss concrete ways of doing this on page 129.
- *Clear objectives and metrics*: implement measurements that leave nothing to chance and make it absolutely unequivocal what has been agreed upon
- *Prompt follow-up*: making sure that you keep track of what has been promised and ask for results in a timely fashion.

The problem can be partly circumvented by making sure that the coworker comes up with the solution by him- or herself, in what is known as a Socratic process. This is of course the generally preferred method of delegation in any company or culture. The manager avoids providing solutions or decisions, and instead tries to "ask the right questions" to ensure that the appropriate final decision is the product of, and has buy-in from, the coworker. Even so, Chinese coworkers will often carefully watch for signs from the boss and try to anticipate desired answers. Careful follow-up remains crucial to success.

Another reason for detailed follow-up is the preoccupation with "face", which often precludes coworkers from flagging potential problems even after they have become apparent to the coworker. Rather than risking being the "bearer of ill tidings", there is a pronounced tendency for coworkers to avoid bringing attention to deviations from the plan until the issues become so large as to be self-evident. Again, this is a frequent source of frustration to expatriate managers in China, who, based on their own background, have different expectations on coworkers.

In China, both of us independently went back to using a management trick from our military service days, where we were taught to always "repeat the order". Asking employees to restate, in their own words, the task and objectives at hand not only ensures clarity and prevents (real or deliberate) misunderstandings, but also makes it easier to avoid linguistic snafus — good to think about in an environment where people tend to answer "yes" to avoid embarrassment even when they have not clearly understood what has just been said. Written meeting notes are another useful way of "repeating the order".

We have also found that group work is an excellent way of ensuring high-quality feedback from subordinates. If you pose a question to an individual, or collectively to a group of 15–20 local employees, you have to be provocative to get any answer or comment. If the same question is asked of smaller groups of three or four people, there will be no end to the vigorous discussions and constructive suggestions that ensue. By "hiding behind the group", the presenter avoids the personal risk of losing face or being seen as stupid. Because of this, groups tend to produce more interesting feedback and ideas than individuals do.

Of course, just as elsewhere in the world, group work also has the added advantage that it results in real buy-in and better ownership than if the same solution had just been provided as an "order". By "asking the right questions" and "asking the question in the right way", group work discussions can provide more than just solutions to concrete issues: the discussion itself tends to cement the group and facilitate subsequent execution. It is therefore imperative that the discussion really focuses on the right issues, which have to be framed carefully beforehand.

7.2.10. *Employees value transparency and fairness*

On page 26, we described guanxi as a lubricant of business transactions, an aspect of the networking abilities and people skills of Chinese coworkers. The flip side of guanxi, and one of the reasons for its remaining importance, is the prevalence of favoritism and nepotism in an environment that lacks clear and objective rules and standards. This is the oft-lamented "rule by personal fiat" and lack of transparency in Chinese organizations.

Chinese coworkers are intensely preoccupied with fairness and transparency in remuneration and promotions. Expatriate managers sometimes see this as a sign of immaturity. This ranking system of Chinese schools teaches young people to view success as a zero-sum game and creates an almost obsessive preoccupation with "fairness". But we also think the desire for objectivity is a natural reaction to the overall trust deficit in Chinese society. Multinational companies are held to high standards and the bright, ambitious recruits that enter their ranks do so precisely because these workplaces are perceived as providing a better environment for potential development than most local competitors.

As a manager, you need to make policies and regulations explicit, and be prepared to rationally defend them, or at least explain them clearly and openly. Salaries, bonuses, and promotion criteria must adhere to a logical, transparent system. This is true even if individual remuneration is supposedly secret — as we will see on page 128, everybody will know each other's salaries anyway.

7.2.11. *The grapevine needs to be actively managed*

The relationship orientation of Chinese employees also means that the informal grapevine is more alive than in other countries where we have worked. Rumors spread quickly. One of us, Anders, went to visit the operations in Guiyang. Anders casually told the local host, the Sales Manager, how good the bean curd was that we had for dinner. When he visited the next Sales Area, Anders was surprised to see identical bean curd on the dinner table. He got similar bean curd in each place he came to on the trip. There are few secrets. Employees talk amongst themselves about their expatriate colleagues — but also about each other.

Managing messages and internal communications are as important as in other countries — but being fast is even more so. The speed of the Chinese grapevine is incredible: close to, but not quite, the speed of light. It has only recently been matched by e-mail and other electronic media. Making sure that internal communications are quickly and accurately managed strengthens internal motivation and avoids unnecessary misunderstandings and conflicts.

7.2.12. *Coworkers tend to adhere to the letter of the law*

Above, we have seen examples of how Chinese business will obfuscate and work around regulations to gain competitive advantage. The same problems will sometimes apply inside your own organization. The root cause is the collapse of moral values during the planned economy of the 1960s and 1970s. There is little loyalty towards large organizations, be they public-sector or corporate.

Company regulations are often interpreted in the most literal way possible. In a Chinese organization, any "benefit" in regulations tends to be interpreted as a "minimum entitlement". In other words, if you do not claim a benefit allowed under the system, whether you have actually incurred it or not, you are simply being naive. Adhering to the letter, rather than the spirit, of the law is not seen as morally reprehensible.

Ernst Behrens, Country Manager of Siemens in China, gave an example of this mentality: "We set up a reimbursement system for travel expenses which stipulated that coworkers could reimburse 'any meal expenses up to 100 RMB'. All our coworkers started claiming exactly 100 RMB of expenses per travel day. And they produced official tax receipts to this precise amount, every time". Similarly, insurance companies complain that policy owners regularly "max out" on allowed reimbursements for purchases of drugs by collecting receipts from family and friends. And if one's own relations fail to provide the necessary proofs of payment, in every Chinese city, there are open-air markets where all kinds of receipts are available for sale.

7.2.13. *There are great cultural differences within China*

A 15th century local chronicle quoted in Mark Elvin's captivating economic history of China, *The Pattern of the Chinese Past*, portrays the area of Wenzhou as it appeared at the time, describing how "the land is poor and unsuitable for growing either lacquer or mulberry trees, yet the locals are well-to-do because they manufacture great quantities of lacquer objects and silk cloth". It is fascinating to observe how, five centuries later, Wenzhou is again China's leading exporter of many kinds of manufactured goods. Regional characteristics are pronounced and rooted in long traditions.

Such regional characteristics give rise to cultural differences, sometimes perceived as even greater than they actually are, within China itself. These differences of course become larger still if one includes in the discussion the other parts of China than the Chinese mainland itself or overseas ethnic Chinese from places like Singapore.

Northern Chinese view Shanghai people as preoccupied with money and lacking in trust. Shanghai people see northerners, particularly Beijing people, as lazy and boorish, and resent the political control that Beijing asserts over what they perceive as the more cosmopolitan and forward Shanghai. Guangzhou people are generally perceived to be down-to-earth and hard-working but not hugely ambitious. Without necessarily endorsing these statements, it is important for managers to acknowledge the differences in perception between Chinese people, because such perceptions often influence management issues and may have a direct bearing on staffing and personal chemistry within teams. Making sure your Beijing and Shanghai offices function smoothly together can be a challenge.

One example is the problem with managers from Hong Kong. In the 1990s, Hong Kong managers were often seen as having a condescending attitude to mainland employees, which frequently created frictions. In general, it has been much harder to get local employees to accept a Hong Kong or Taiwan expatriate manager than a Westerner. This is not a "racial" issue — American- or European-born Chinese tend to be well accepted. We believe it is more of a cultural problem. One of the attractions of working for a multinational is the chance to learn from global experience and system. Hong Kong managers have often been seen as "too Chinese" to provide this environment, but yet "not Chinese enough" to be well versed in the local mainland market and culture. These problems seem to be less pronounced nowadays.

7.3. Find the Best Candidates, Trust Them, Train Them, and Promote Them

Building a strong and successful organization in any country or industry depends on recruiting, training, and retaining the best employees. Due to the size and fluidity of its human resources market, China is an extreme illustration of this universal principle, but cultural prejudices sometimes get in the way of best management practices.

7.3.1. *Recruitment in China is like panning for gold*

The typical Theory X China manager will remind you that "there are 1.3 billion people in China — if you don't like your job, there are plenty of others who do". This statement actually holds some truth in a recruitment situation. But the implication is actually the opposite of what the speaker typically means: we actually need to be unusually disciplined and careful when recruiting in China.

As we have seen, we believe China is a "human resource-scarce" market, and will probably remain so for a long time. This means that out of the thousands of job applications that a multinational receives every month, only a few are worth considering. In other words, the choice is large, so one must devise accurate methods of screening large numbers of CV's, some of which will themselves be of dubious accuracy.

One of us recently received a call from a large multinational that had received an application from a former receptionist at our company. They were asking if we could provide a reference and verify the accuracy of the CV. As it was faxed over, it became clear that this receptionist had played a much larger role at our company than we had realized. As "assistant to the General Manager" and "responsible for office management at the Beijing office of a major multinational with 100+ employees", this 22-year-old had ostensibly been in charge of "managing hospitality and catering" (which we remembered as serving coffee to office visitors) as well as "General Manager schedule and travel arrangements" (buying air tickets and booking hotels) and "internal communications" (routing phone calls).

One might of course credit the former receptionist with eloquent creativity and a commendable go-get-it attitude, if it were not for the fact that the English and general style of the CV also made it evident that it had been written by someone else.

In this particular case, the new employer was actually behaving in an unusually professional way. Reference calls are surprisingly uncommon, given that our own HR Managers frequently find not only elaborations of the truth, but also false university degrees and spurious statements of work experience on applications. It is important to provide a backup check on any applicant. Do not assume that your headhunter has done so.

Once you have satisfied yourself regarding the applicant's previous experience, you need to take them through a structured interview process. We have successfully used personality profiling using PAPI and DISC psychometrics tools of each candidate when we came towards the final interviews — and there are many other alternatives available. Chinese colleagues tend to be enthusiastic about such tests, as it gives them an unusual chance for introspection and self-reflection. Apart from providing us with pertinent information, these tests have therefore also proven a valuable tool during the final discussions with the candidates: Based on the questionnaire results, interesting questions were brought to the surface. But as any manager knows, such tests must of course never be used as a standalone tool for accepting or refusing a candidate — they are, at best, good discussion starters and a complement and aid in making an overall appraisal of the candidate.

Perhaps the single most important learning, shared by managers in every country and culture is that you make your biggest mistakes when you do not follow your gut reaction, your instincts. This is where the language problem comes back to haunt the Western manager — when you recruit someone, how can you judge their character and personal style when talking to them in a language that is not their native tongue (and perhaps not yours, either)?

As your organization grows, one way to solve this problem is to involve people you trust in the selection process. Both of us have made a practice of applying what is often called the "grandfather principle": letting the recruiting manager make the final choice — but with a veto possibility from the senior manager.

To be successful in recruitment in China, you must:

- *Spread your net wide*: The right candidate is out there — but he or she can be more difficult to find than in a more mature economy. For senior positions, you may have to think out of the box to find the right candidate.
- *Do background checks*: It is common to find spurious claims and even fake documentation in job applications. Checking up on

the background of an employee can be difficult and may even require special investigations in the case of senior candidates.

- *Be fast*: You also have to be aware of the fact that competent managers have so much more choice in the marketplace than they would in more mature economies. This means that the best candidates will disappear quickly, so you must make sure that your own recruitment process, no matter how rigorous, moves forward quickly from first contact to final offer.
- *Sell the job*: It is incumbent on you and your company to attract the recruit. Be prepared to give concrete and specific answers to questions on personal development and education/training.
- *Trust your instincts*: We cannot repeat it too often: do not hire somebody in China that you would not hire in your home country.
- *Recognize and act on hiring mistakes*: Chinese employment law still allows for flexibility in hiring and firing. This means you should immediately take action if you realize that you may have made a wrong hire. At the same time, keep in mind that even if hiring and firing meets few legal obstacles, your own colleagues will of course want such decisions communicated and explained to them.

7.3.2. *Hiring on coworker recommendations*

Current employees can, as in most countries, be an excellent source of candidates for the company, with one caveat: As we have seen, the Chinese guanxi system and warm care for one's immediate relations makes it perfectly natural for some people to recommend close friends, relatives, even spouses, for a job. It is therefore important that recommendations are vetted and that potential hires are put through the same rigorous application process as other candidates.

In order to encourage coworkers to "cast their nets wide", a finder's fee or bonus can be useful. To avoid potential embarrassment and loss of face, make sure to communicate clearly that it is an interview opportunity, not a guaranteed job, that is on offer.

7.3.3. *Promote young people by localizing your organization*

We have argued that, if you treat them right, your local coworkers will guarantee your success on the Chinese market. By showing commitment, you can keep short-term temptations to jump ship. But if you want your high-flyer local colleagues to stay on for the really long term you also need to provide a clear promotion path that will motivate them to do so. Providing a successful promotion path entails more than just spelling out future job roles. If you continuously bring in expatriate or other external recruits at higher positions in the company, local colleagues may start to doubt their own chances of promotion or even perceive a "glass ceiling" blocking local talent from reaching top jobs. This can be detrimental to motivation and morale.

The long-term business success of any company in China will depend on the success of its localization strategy — in other words, how you manage to identify and nurture local management talent. There are pressures on multinational companies to localize: expatriate packages are expensive, in many industries prohibitively so, and local managers may be better at interacting with Chinese customers and authorities.

But localization can also be challenging. As we have seen, there is a severe shortage of experienced managers in China, and this shortage will not let up anytime soon. This means you will have to promote younger, less experienced people in China than you may be used to from other markets. This will not be unique for your company. Young people are the movers and shakers in China today, as borne out by statistics on personal income: 30-somethings have higher salaries than any other age group in the country. There are of course clear advantages to promoting younger colleagues:

- Young colleagues are flexible, adaptable, and ambitious.
- Junior employees will have started earlier in their careers at your company and will be well steeped in your culture — you can avoid legacy problems and "bad habits" from other organizations.

But promoting young, relatively inexperienced people is also fraught with challenges. Doing this successfully requires a clear plan and strong systems that can provide direction and guidance. In particular, you need to:

- *Provide hands-on leadership, role modeling, and mentoring*: Your typical recruit will be highly motivated and keen to learn, but will lack experience and "big picture" business context. If you manage your young recruits well, and provide them with good role models, they are also malleable. You can shape the way your organization will look a few years down the line.
- *Provide extensive training*: Recruits tend to be receptive to formal training and personal development opportunities; these will therefore influence retention and team stability as well as efficiency.
- *Manage expectations*: Young managers sometimes have an overly optimistic assessment of their own abilities. Managing expectations and avoiding "promotion to the point of incompetence" can become a real challenge. As we have seen, you will also need to manage the expectations of less high-flying colleagues.

Providing mentoring and support without stifling individual initiative is a difficult art. There are no shortcuts — you need to put in considerable face time with mentees to get the desired long-term effects — but we have also been able to put in place systems that have helped us accomplish these goals.

Providing new challenges can be a way of managing expectations and laying the groundwork for a more accurate self-assessment by a young ambitious individual. BASF's Jöerg Wuttke works actively with job rotations between geographies and business areas: "This gets people out of their silos. We will take a guy who is great in Nanjing and put him in Shenyang. If he does a good job there too, we send him to Japan or Korea. It puts the young manager in a position to better understand German colleagues: 'the food is different, my wife cannot move'".

Perhaps the most successful method in our experience is the "regular visitor system". Instead of providing a full-time mentor, we have tried to identify older, experienced people from the international organization that can take on a "part-time" mentoring responsibility for high-potential local recruits. The person will typically travel regularly to China and stay with the mentee for two to four weeks. This system has a number of advantages.

- It is usually easy to find candidates. We have tried to find managers who, in a downsizing situation, may be "past their prime" in their own organization, but who still have a lot of experience to contribute to a young mentee. By offering to pay part of the person's salary, we are taking a burden off the home organization, meaning they will often be cooperative. Since the mentorship does not necessitate moving permanently to China, it also becomes easier to handle for spouses and families.
- The method is relatively inexpensive. Conversely, moving a senior expatriate to China usually entails providing housing, schooling for children, special allowances, and other ancillary expenses.
- Perhaps most importantly, the method makes for better mentoring since the mentee person is free of the mentor most of the time. There is little risk of the mentee seeing the mentor as a threat to their independence, and it forces the mentee to take his or her own decisions during the periods when the mentor is absent.

In implementing this system, we have seen an almost total rate of satisfaction from all parties concerned. We will discuss a particularly successful application in the chapter on building and developing the sales force.

7.3.4. *Salaries should start low and increase rapidly*

The implications for salary structures in a resource-scarce market are also clear: because of the lack of senior people, the salaries of young people rise quickly as they gain experience. Chinese employees will expect to be rapidly promoted and to see fast salary growth. Western, particularly European, firms tend to have too small pay differentiation between juniors and seniors; by paying too much for entry-level recruits they make it harder to provide fast and high-percentage salary raises, and by paying too little for experienced employees, particularly those who have grown with the company, they easily lose the most valuable employees to poaching by competitors.

Failing to keep up-to-date with labor market trends can be expensive. Developments have been particularly evident in starting salaries for university graduates. At the beginning of the 21st century, large groups of fresh university graduates found themselves without work for the first time since the launch of the economic reform policies in the 1980s. The situation is the same for returnee MBA's without current on-the-ground experience from China; entry-level salaries have deteriorated rapidly because companies tend to value real business experience and track record more than academic achievements. Smart graduates are starting to choose jobs that can help them build a career, rather than going for highest bidders.

At the same time, salary ranges have not yet settled into clear industry standards. In our work with different multinationals, we have seen examples where, for similar work, employees in one manufacturing company will be making perhaps 3,000 RMB, at another 7,000–10,000 RMB, and where the same work role may command up to 15,000 RMB at an American representative office. According to annual salary surveys conducted by HR companies such as Hewitt Associates, American companies tend to pay more than European ones, and representative offices pay more than "real" companies do. Does that mean American companies are generally doing better or making more money in China than German ones (who, according to the surveys, pay less)? We do not believe it is so. In fact, we do not even see that paying more influences companies' overall abilities to attract top talent in the market. "We pay according to our structure and others pay according to their structure — but we don't seem to recruit better people just because we pay better", a disillusioned American manager commented to us.

As we have seen, the demographics of pay are also inverted compared to most other countries. Because of China's recent history, young people actually make more money than older people and you will find unusually young people in senior positions. An entire generation was lost during the cultural revolution when universities closed and managerial careers were limited to state jobs. In today's China, most 30-somethings are making higher salaries than their parents.

Because of the lack of consistency on the market, a consistent salary system *within* your own company becomes crucial. As long as employees see a clear rationale for their salaries and those of their peers, and as long as they see a clear path to promotion and salary raises, they will be less likely to compare themselves to employees of other companies. Some companies have tried to keep salaries secret by having regulations that prohibit employees from disclosing what they earn, but this is a no-starter in China. Employees are intensely curious about the salaries, benefits, and bonuses of their colleagues, and will go to great lengths to ferret them out. Whereas asking a person about his or her salary in the West is often seen as a breach of privacy, it is perfectly alright to do so in China. You can be absolutely certain that most of your employees will have a clear picture of how their own salaries compare to those around them, and they will often let you know during salary negotiations.

As we have seen above, Chinese coworkers are also preoccupied with the perceived fairness of the remuneration system. In our experience, the key is having a clear salary structure within one's company and adhering to this rigorously. It is far more important that your employees perceive your own system as internally fair than that your average salaries match those of your competitors.

7.3.5. *Offer competitive but fair titles*

Local colleagues do not just discuss salaries — they also compare titles. The face that a good title confers is more important in China than in the West. Junior employees, in particular, will often tell you that they have difficulties facing their friends and old schoolmates if they cannot boast of a title that matches those of their peers. They will also compare themselves to colleagues in other departments, and even across organizations, complaining that others with higher titles are doing the same job as they are.

Just as with salaries, it is therefore imperative that titles are conferred in a consistent way throughout the local organization, and according to as objective criteria as possible. Many companies, international and local, are quite liberal with titles — after all, there is no additional cost in conferring a somewhat higher title. Still, a word of caution is warranted. Title inflation is a workable, sometimes even necessary, strategy, but taken too far it risks devaluing the reputation of your own organization as an employer. If titles are too high, people simply see through them: at Eastwei, we often have recruits who are willing to step down a notch or two in order to join what is perceived to be "a better company". Compared to the opportunity to learn and grow, titles are still less important.

Some multinationals have adopted the rather sneaky approach of translating bland Western titles into more attractive Chinese versions: "Managers" become "Directors" or even "VP's" in translation. This particular shade of title inflation generally seems to work well.

7.3.6. *Involve employees in the decision-making process*

We have seen that local coworkers display some characteristics that can make it difficult to implement management decisions. They are, for example, often fiercely individualistic, and they will avoid openly confronting decisions even when they do not agree, instead choosing to subvert implementation through inaction. Junior managers will also avoid making difficult decisions, especially if these risk alienating colleagues.

Anders encountered these problems frequently when opening new sales offices. Sandvik is made up of separate divisions; what promised to be an excellent location for one division was not necessarily so for another one. A divisional manager who agreed to a location in a less than ideal city would face the prospect of going back to the division head and explaining their choice. When we opened offices in big and "obvious" cities there were few problems, but when we started to open in second- and third-tier cities, the problems occurred. We faced a lot of guerilla warfare from disgruntled managers who were reluctant to bring bad news back to the divisions.

This problem was solved by introducing management groups, where functional managers were asked to take wider responsibilities for the business as a whole. The idea was to counteract silo mentality and foster teamwork and cooperation by involving groups of managers in decisions. We also continuously reinforced the concept that you participate in the management group not only as a representative of your group, but also more importantly as a representative of the total company. We found that implementation became faster when the decision-making process became more transparent to the individual manager:

- It became easier for managers to accept those decisions that were not perfectly aligned with their own interests, but were still for the good of the company as a whole.
- Managers were able to "tell" the story from a company perspective: in the decision-making process, they were automatically furnished with convincing arguments for why this decision was the right one at the company level. This in turn allowed them to "sell" the story to their colleagues in the divisions.

By forming a cross-functional management group, it is possible to foster a climate where individual managers take responsibility for the company as a whole. In the management group the leaders participate. Even though functional managers represent their own functions in the management group — be they sales, production, or whatever — they also collectively represent the whole company.

For Chinese coworkers, this can be a new and challenging experience. The trick is to force the manager out of his or her box, leaving no alternative than saying "we decided" instead of "they decided". Some managers were reluctant to take part, but in the end the management groups turned out not only to be good for short-term execution of the decisions made: once managers broke out of their reluctance for participating in difficult decisions, coworkers and subordinates tended to respect them even more. It is surprisingly common in China to hear managers giving orders to their subordinates declaring that "our GM says that...". This, of course, does not engender respect, in China or elsewhere. Taking responsibility for all decisions, not just the pleasant ones, builds esteem for a manager. But in China, managers often need support in doing this.

The management group process needs to be carefully controlled so that participating managers do not feel they have simply been "taken hostage". Objections need to be taken seriously and discussed in depth. In the case of the sales office location problem, we handled the most acute complaints by drafting a 3-year plan, in which most needs could be met — albeit some before others.

7.3.7. *Formal training is a key factor in retaining Chinese coworkers*

We have already stressed the importance of offering formal training to Chinese employees. The stress here is on "formal". Employers all over the world recognize the importance of developing coworkers through an ongoing process of on-the-job training; in this context, they emphasize the *usefulness* or *applicability* of the new knowledge or skills. In China, training must ideally also be perceived to be a real investment that yields tangible "academic" as well as "practical" results. Formal training should ideally be part of an ongoing program and be rewarded with some form of a degree or a certificate. Usually, this kind of training will be externally sourced, or handled at a special training center in China or abroad.

We have already mentioned some of the characteristics of Chinese employees that make the formal aspect so important in China:

- They are impatient and want to be able to see their own progress from day to day (or at least quarter to quarter).
- They have an ingrained respect for academic achievement, based in millennia of Chinese history.
- They see investments in training as proof of the company's commitment to their own career.
- They value the "face" of being able to tell family and friends how much the company is investing in them.

To feel that one is getting the necessary "tools" for doing a good job, is another essential factor. Here, of course, training plays an important role. Often this training has to be done more fundamentally and covering more areas than we are used to do in the West, where we often have a workforce with more experience. Most of the training must of course be done locally in China, but it is important also for more senior staff with longer service that they get training at headquarters and that this training period is used to let them see the operations in locations outside China as well as develop personal relationships with management there. The response to training abroad is normally very positive. The fact that our local people make contacts and friends at the parent company means that their roots grow deeper and they become more reluctant to leave.

Our colleague Per Dahl, a senior management trainer with years of global experience, emphasizes the high motivation of local employees: "It is incredibly fun to teach in China — people are so receptive and open to learning new skills and ways of thinking".

Anders had the same experience. In the beginning, before Anders's parent company got used to how ambitious our local employees really are, we always got very positive feedback, when we sent people there for training: "they are all sitting in the first row listening and taking notes all the time". Their good personal behavior also drew a lot of positive comments, contrasting drastically to that of some participants from other countries.

Training should include cultural aspects such as how to interact with expatriate managers. Local employees must be given cultural, not just technical, skills to interact with the international organization.

Although we emphasize the formal aspect of training in China, the usual rules of course still apply: To ensure maximum benefit, training should be provided after some initial work experience is gained, in areas where the employee is well motivated, and with sufficient follow-up and coordination with incentive systems to make sure that knowledge is actually retained.

At Eastwei, we discovered that motivation and learning actually increased if we told coworkers explicitly how much the session cost, calculated on a per-person basis. Few employees imagine that costs of hiring a teacher, renting the venue, and transporting colleagues from around the country for a one- or two-day training course can easily amount to thousands of RMB per student and day. If this cost is made explicit, student commitment increases.

Chapter 8
The Right Corporate Culture

In the last chapter, we looked at some unique aspects of working in China and outlined ways of dealing with them from an operational perspective. Let us now move up one level of abstraction and ask ourselves some follow-up questions: How relatively important are cultural differences really in business? How much do companies need to adapt to a unique Chinese reality? And what are the lessons for cross-cultural management in a globalized world?

8.1. You cannot Fake It

In the 1990s, Johan was a young manager, on his own in a strange country trying to build a company with two empty hands. How should he manage his fledgling organization to make it successful in China? His own observations seemed to bear out what Chinese colleagues continuously told him: local employees were irresponsible, needed careful supervision and controls and clear lines of authority. They responded best to economic incentives such as bonuses directly tied to short-term performance or the completion of specific tasks.

Johan was also told that as a manager in China, it is important to establish authority. His own corner office was four times as large as the partitions provided to other employees and it was, of course, carefully guarded by his trusty secretary.

His company Eastwei muddled along. Sure, it grew, as any company tends to grow when the overall economic environment is ticking away at an annual 10% or so of GDP growth, but there was nothing particularly impressive about it compared to the competition. Employee loyalty and retention was also roughly the same as those of competitors — the best people tended to stay for a couple of years, the less capable for a bit longer.

Then, in 1998, a few senior employees tendered their resignations within a few weeks of each other. Johan felt an acute sense of crisis — since the "production facilities" of a consulting company are made up entirely of brains rather than fixed assets such as machinery, losing employees is equivalent to seeing your factory being dismantled and carried away by competitors. Continuously starting from scratch like this just could not be the right way to run a successful company.

In order to find out where the problem was, Johan conducted in-depth interviews with every employee in the organization. As he talked to more and more coworkers, a picture emerged. And it turned out this picture could have been equally well painted in a Western company in London, Stockholm, or New York.

Perhaps the results of Johan's mini survey were most interesting because they were so commonplace. It turns out employees were looking to be better informed and to participate more in company decisions; they wanted to be more empowered, were looking for a clearer overall vision and less micro management. Not exactly rocket science for a modern manager.

By reinventing the company culture, we achieved a transformation that made Eastwei the fastest-growing PR agency in China. Out went the partitions — and the boss' corner office! We also threw out a lot of the hierarchical structures that supposedly were so important in China and created a more modern, team-based structure. We spent time actively discussing the company's culture and vision — what kind of an organization we wanted to be. We de-emphasized individual bonuses and performance salaries and instead instituted group bonuses. These reforms were so painful that some of our best remaining employees threatened to walk out: "How can we do PR without our own private space" and "why should I share my bonus with lower performers" were typical comments. Some coworkers tried to deflect the changes by questioning how Johan, as the boss, could work without his own office for "secret conversations".

In the end, we managed to persuade the team to try the new work style on one condition: we would go with the changes for three months, and if protests remained, we would roll them back. The result: increased teamwork, lower employee turnover, and vastly improved client service. Even our new business pipeline grew as rainmakers felt stronger support from their teams who could start benefiting from group bonuses. After three months, not a single voice was raised for rolling back our management innovations.

This experience illustrates a key learning for any manager in China: there is no "Chinese" way of managing a company. Although we try to provide some tips on specific issues in this book, the basis for success must come from staying true to your heart and to your company's best practices, your company culture. But the ramifications of company culture go even further. We believe a strong company culture can be perhaps *the* most important competitive asset in China.

8.2. Culture is Especially Important in China

During the 1990s, the claim that "China is different" was a mantra constantly repeated by expatriates and local employees alike. People who made their living by interpreting this ostensible cultural gap and how it should be handled, had vested interests in pointing out and sometimes exaggerating differences.

Of course China is different. It is actually very different, if one wants to focus on differences. But if one wants to look for similarities, these are just as many. For one thing, business challenges are similar regardless of culture. Every business person will say that "people are our most important asset"; you need to build a solid foundation of good people and practices based on an accurate perception of the market information in order to achieve sustainable development.

But similarities are greater than differences when it comes to people management as well. Similarities are obviously most pronounced in the fundamental needs of human beings, while differences stem from (relatively) more superficial value systems and from the dynamics of society — overall level of development, social security, mobility, and so on. Employees — human beings — all want to have a reasonable salary and working conditions, feel a sense of belonging and respect, and feel that they have the chance to develop their careers and influence their future. Differences, on the other hand, tend to revolve around *how* to achieve these deeper goals.

When Anders set out to rapidly expand the Sandvik business in China, he tried to implement "Western management with Chinese characteristics" (to paraphrase Deng Xiaoping's description of the "socialist market economy" that the leadership was trying to build in China). In other words, the fundamentals of the way the company did business and interacted with its employees would remain unchanged, but the development of society and the influences from Chinese culture would be taken into account in implementing this culture. Implementing the corporate culture, values, and loyalty that you have in other parts of the world can be hard work in China. Indeed, as time passed, Anders spent more and more time making sure that the culture was expressed in a way that made it clear, explicit, and possible to grasp for all employees.

So, why spend time building and making explicit a corporate culture? Why not just follow the old adage "when in Rome, do as the Romans do"? Why is retaining your global corporate culture so important in China? There are several reasons:

- Culture does more than just enhance long-term company results — it directly influences efficiency and thus the short-term bottom line. In China, your company will usually be growing fast. Growth is difficult to manage in any market — too many inexperienced coworkers will bring growing pains in the form of miscommunication, lack of familiarity with processes, lack of initiative in grey areas where the usual processes may not apply, and so on. There will be lots of new individuals who must be quickly assimilated and introduced to the way your company does business. A strong culture speeds up this process. A strong corporate culture is also a symbol telling new coworkers that the company has direction, stability and is disciplined about the way it does business.

- In a developed marketplace, there is a wide pool of technically qualified potential employees. It is relatively easy to replace a cog in the corporate machinery: "If things don't suit you, just leave. There are plenty of people who want your job". But in a market like China, were qualified recruits are in chronically short supply, the reply to this comment would be: "Yes, but not very good ones. And even fewer who speak reasonably good English. And hardly anyone with experience. And certainly not colleagues who know and understand your company and its business in-depth". In a world of rapid change and opportunities that seem endless, attracting and keeping the best employees becomes especially important. A strong and unique culture can differentiate your company from your competitors, contributing to your attractiveness as an employer by providing a sense of identity that other companies lack. We all want to feel proud of our job — of what we achieve and of the company we work for. A strong corporate culture emphasizing our company's high standards and values, as well as the quality of the products and services that we sell, nurtures this pride.

- As the Chinese society is transformed, traditional values are in flux. The lack of spirituality also leads young people to look for emotional and social security. Coworkers often work hard, and the work-life balance has been heavily skewed in favor of the workplace. The tendency is therefore to see the workplace as equally important to one's family and friends. If the company culture can provide the stability and guidance that coworkers are looking for, this will also serve to retain those employees that best identify with your way of doing things.

- Employees have a different educational background and world outlook than those in countries that have traditionally been more open to the outside world. Although the young generation of Chinese are much better informed and open to the world around them, barriers to understanding, not least from language, are still high. A clearly expressed framework of company culture makes it easier to adapt to change, especially rapid change.

Company culture is not something that "just happens" — it has been built over years, sometimes decades. In more mature markets, the culture will be in the walls. In China, this culture must be actively nurtured in order to blend into and support your global culture. By "global culture", we do not necessarily mean you should import the good with the bad, wholesale. For example, local employees sometimes complain that decision making is too slow at Western companies — surely, increasing speed is a competitive advantage that becomes especially salient on the hyper-competitive local market. But you do need to retain the cultural traits that make your company unique and which can be harnessed as competitive advantages. It is up to you, as a manager, to identify and nurture these aspects of corporate culture while gently adapting them to the Chinese reality.

The importance of culture as a competitive advantage will increase in other markets that share the Chinese characteristics of rapid change and hyper-competition. Michael Treschow, Chairman of Unilever and Ericsson, convincingly made this point in a speech on globalization in Beijing. Treschow, who has long experience of overseeing substantial businesses in China in his present capacities and previously as CEO of Electrolux, the world's largest household appliance maker, mentioned some of the China factors that are becoming more important for companies in a globally competitive environment: "Corporate culture must be about more than just the usual 'we focus on the customer and on providing quality product' — people are becoming the most important competitive advantage and people need to have a sense of mission and belonging... A strong corporate culture leads to trust and to necessary simplification of processes, allowing companies to move more swiftly as the pace of competition speeds up". Treschow went on to mention, from a global viewpoint, several of the factors that we will be discussing from a Chinese perspective.

So, given that we believe company culture is a key success factor on the Chinese market, what are the implications for managers? What, exactly, is "culture"? And how can we actively build and maintain it?

8.3. Invest Heavily Upfront

Perhaps the most important conclusion to be drawn from the importance of building a strong, clearly enunciated company culture is this: investments, especially of managerial time and commitment, must be what we call "top-heavy". By this we mean that significant capacity should be invested at the very outset of operations in China, in order to provide the local organization with a "culture transfusion" that can serve as a model for the behavior of fresh employees.

One of us was involved for several years with a venture that serves as a clear illustration — and warning. In the early 1990s, a Fortune-500 multinational company had just acquired a major production facility in an inland city of China with some 3000 employees from a state-owned Chinese enterprise. A successful European manager with a strong track record in establishing high-quality manufacturing operations was sent out to manage and transform the venture. The initial monthly conference calls were upbeat — the local coworkers were hard-working, supportive and committed to making things happen. The partner was helpful. Operations would soon commence and product was scheduled to hit the market "in a couple of months".

However, as the conference calls continued, more and more action points were carried over from previous meetings and started piling up at the end of the meeting minutes. The tone of the discussion also changed tangibly. Suggestions from corporate management were increasingly met with skepticism from the local manager: "I'm not sure the partner would agree to that" or "I don't think we have the necessary human resources" would be the typical explanations offered for the continued delays.

It was soon apparent that the manager was facing huge inertia from the local organization and could accomplish little on his own. A factory manager, then a quality control person, and a financial manager were sent out for support. Production was now a year behind schedule. The corporate Board started grumbling. More managers were sent out, but since expatriate salaries (at the time including hefty hardship allowances, apartment rents and even a private chauffeur for each expatriated employee) were high, this caused costs to skyrocket, with further lack of confidence as a result. In the end, 18 months behind the original timetable, production finally got started. The original manager left soon afterwards, but ten years later the company was still suffering from the problems provoked by the early failure to provide adequate management resources for the operation. This story also illustrates some of the more general problems with joint ventures, which are dealt with in more detail in Chapter 6.

Contrast this with the way the most successful companies build their China operations. When IKEA opened its Beijing store in 1998, observers were struck by the large number of expatriate employees teeming around the construction site. At the peak of activity, there was one foreigner, experienced from a mature IKEA operation abroad, for every two local employees. The fledgling employees thus had ongoing access to knowledge and experience — but also to role models that could steep them in the IKEA "way". The expatriate employees similarly received support and reassurance by being part of a strong team of peers.

The opening of an IKEA store is, of course an extreme example, where business goes from zero to several hundred million RMB in one fell swoop. But even for businesses that grow along a more smooth trajectory, ramping up expatriates faster than business volume at the beginning of local market activities and then gradually removing them as the organization matures is usually the best strategy.

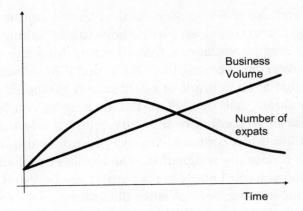

By sending in a lot of manpower at the beginning of a China venture, and then gradually removing the expatriates as the organization matures, successful companies create a strong platform for success. Initial salary costs should be seen as an investment rather than as "running costs" or "headcount". Although the initial overhead for expatriate managers and experts are high, head office, board and stock market are happy when these costs gradually decrease as the local organization matures and can take on greater responsibilities.

8.4. Actively Develop the Culture

Corporate culture does not just "appear" — it is the result of a long-term process of events, experiences, symbols, and signals. Most of these can be actively managed. There are of course some obvious elements that contribute to a strong culture:

- Senior management setting the example and becoming strong role models by displaying their own force of character.
- Senior management consistency — never (never ever, not a single time) departing from your fundamental principles.
- Salary and bonus systems that reinforce desired behavior.

But there are also ways to work actively with culture-building. These range from training and workshops to storytelling and even proactively staging situations that illustrate how the culture is applied in everyday working life. The "failed IBM salesman" story is often quoted as an example of a deliberately promoted corporate myth to illustrate that "it's OK to fail, as long as you learn from your mistakes". According to the story, a junior salesman at IBM failed a million-dollar contract with a key customer and went to his manager to tender his resignation. The manager replied: "Under no circumstances will I allow you to quit. I just invested a million bucks in your training, son!" A story illustrating a service-oriented corporate culture is the old "deliberate delivery of faulty product" saw, where the company sends a complex piece of machinery with a small component missing, in order to be able to immediately helicopter in their service person as a demonstration of commitment to the customer.

On page 142, we saw how one of us applied staging as a way of establishing and fostering a culture of open, straightforward communication in his company.

8.5. Do Not Rush Localization

In the first years of the 21st century, a multinational Fortune-500 company decided to localize its China management to ensure that the local company would be led by people with a deep understanding of the local market. The company appointed a Beijing-born but internationally savvy manager, a charming and verbal ivy-league graduate, to head up its China operations. Within one year, the new GM replaced all expatriate staff but one with hand-picked Chinese employees, the stated objective being to reduce operating costs by saving on expatriate salaries. During the first two or three

(Continued)

(Continued)

years, business results were looking good, and confidence at head office grew. Still, there were people who had their doubts. "Our China GM is hard to get a grip on", his newly appointed direct boss at headquarters told Johan. "He actually seems a bit slippery. Is this a Chinese thing?" In spite of Johan's assurances that this was definitely not "a Chinese thing" and that it would be wise to allay such suspicions through more hands-on involvement from head office, the country manager remained in place. When business results collapsed a couple of years later, it turned out that the local manager had built a miniature private empire, unknown to his colleagues at head office, which had siphoned off millions of dollars through spurious deals with his corporate employer.

As we have seen, a successful localization strategy — identifying and nurturing local management talent — will determine the long-term profitability and ultimate success of most multinationals in China. Expatriate packages are expensive; local managers may be better at interacting with Chinese customers and authorities; and public opinion in China has, from time to time, scrutinized multinationals who have been perceived to have a glass ceiling for local employees.

In view of these pressures, some multinationals have localized too quickly. The results of under-managed localization can be severe: lack of coherence in the local organization, rapidly declining business results and in some cases a lack of control leading to corruption and other serious problems.

A successful localization strategy needs to be carefully planned and managed with a long-term perspective. Successful companies localize only when their local people are mature enough. And successful managers, especially in China, never forget that their primary role is that of mentoring new talent and developing the local organization.

8.6. Guard Against Corruption

In the box in the preceding section, we gave an example of one of the results of ill-managed localization: corruption. Corruption has been systemic in China during much of the country's history. In older times, provincial officials were expected to provide for themselves partially through bribes. Corruption is more pervasive in China than in many other countries where companies do business. In 2007, Transparency International, an authoritative international organization to combat corruption, ranked China 72 out of 180 countries, where 180 was the most corrupt.

The way business is done also differs between China and the West. Go to any market for a crash course in local business ethics: as a Westerner, you will be offered an opening price of, say, 450 RMB for a "guaranteed pure silk" shirt; after negotiations you pay less than the material cost if the shirt were really silk. A Westerner would often feel awkward opening at such an obviously ridiculous price. Similarly, some local suppliers find it perfectly natural to offer a kickback to a presumptive buyer from a corporate purchasing department. Cultural acceptance of such bribes is so high that it will usually take greater effort to negotiate a 15% discount than a 15% kickback from a vendor.

This means that there is a lot of under-the-table wheeling and dealing going on even in multinational companies. We are not talking about isolated problems at individual companies. Although information can only be anecdotal, we are personally aware of many cases, ranging from the secretary who accepts a percentage on flight tickets and office supplies, to the country General Manager embezzling millions of dollars. For an employee to embezzle large amounts from a multinational corporation is relatively risk-free. Even if the person is discovered, company management will usually be reluctant to press charges because of the draconian Chinese legal system; few Western companies will risk sending a colleague to death row, regardless of the amount of money involved.

Is this a major management problem, or just a cost of doing business in China? Let us look at how corruption influences the organizations of multinationals in the country.

There are two different kinds of corruption in business: the bribes or favors that companies provide in order to generate sales or obtain policy favors, and corruption that means companies themselves pay more than they should to vendors who have strong personal relationships within their own organization.

Nearly all Western companies in China will try to control their own purchasing process. Clearly, having your employees accept kickbacks from vendors is unacceptable. Some companies, however, tacitly acknowledge the need for providing kickbacks to customers as a necessary component of doing business in China: "Everyone else in our industry pays kickbacks, so if we want to do business in China, we have no choice". Companies who are too careful to pay bribes on their own sometimes arrange elaborate agreements with Chinese "agents" who can sell the goods, no questions asked. In discussions with Western business people, one sometimes even gets the impression that paying kickbacks is seen as a "cool" or "inside" thing to do — it is just that little bit exotic.

How should one handle the legal, ethical and business dilemma of illegal payments and bribes? Let us state at the very outset that we believe it is possible, in almost every industry, to do business in China without paying kickbacks. Both of us have been exposed to the dilemma of whether or not to pay kickbacks to customers. In these cases, it was made clear to us that we would lose the business if we could not pay a kickback. In some cases, that has indeed happened. But in our view, the business lost has, almost by definition, been of a "lower quality" than the business won in fair competition. By keeping your company to higher standards and winning your business by virtue of a better offering, greater skill or professionalism, you create a stronger, more competitive organization. We thus both, independently of each other and in different industries, came to the conclusion that keeping our organizations clean of corruption does come at a short-term price in terms of lost business, but that the long-term benefits far outweigh these costs.

It is also becoming increasingly difficult for multinational companies to employ unethical business practices, including kickbacks. One reason is the healthy scrutiny from NGO's. But perhaps the greatest force for change is the rapidly transforming Chinese business landscape. As private enterprise becomes more important, the opportunities for corruption are shrinking. After all, your customers, too, live in a fiercely competitive world and increasingly want to get the best deal possible from every supplier.

The battle against corruption is a high priority for the Chinese government. Taking a firm stand against corrupt practices is not only the right thing to do for multinationals in the country; it also makes good business sense.

8.6.1. *How to keep your organization clean*

Clearly, corruption is a major management challenge. Apart from the obvious, potentially serious, legal consequences — corruption is, of course, illegal in China — it creates misalignments inside the organization. The financial costs to companies may not always be that great — one may sometimes argue that the company would be paying the same price for goods whether or not a kickback is paid. But corruption will often become gradually apparent to other employees than those involved, and will therefore quickly feed rumors that eat away at company culture and confidence. Corruption is contagious, also in the sense that it is difficult to keep your own organization clean if at the same time the company (perhaps tacitly) allows kickbacks to customers. It is not uncommon for sales people of multinationals to share kickbacks with individuals in the customer organization; this can create pricing problems that are almost impossible to correct.

We also need to realize that it is not always easy for our local employees to stay away from kickbacks. Not only are there constant temptations — vendors actively suggest kickbacks to your coworkers — but there are also pressures. Chinese people are keen to take care of friends and family. Pressure from a relative for a chance to sell to your company can be much harder to refuse than an ordinary bribe. It is up to the manager to limit the temptations, opportunities, and pressures that employees may be subject to.

Western managers are naive when it comes to corruption. We do not think a good manager should constantly suspect his coworkers of misdemeanor, but a healthy dose of paranoia will, to paraphrase Andy Grove, the famous Intel CEO, certainly help companies survive in the Chinese marketplace. It is therefore useful to be aware of some of the typical ways that multinational companies are cheated in China.

- Sales persons can skim profits from their company by setting up a sales company, sometimes in the name of a wife, husband, or other relative, and selling company products at a discounted price to this "customer" for subsequent re-sale to the real customers. We have seen at least three such cases in the companies we have worked with, and other managers tell similar stories. This kind of scam can involve enormous amounts of money.
- Marketing managers giving business to advertising agencies or PR consultants where they themselves, directly or indirectly, have equity or other forms of indirect control; in such cases, they are sure to have a stake in the profits. Of course, kickbacks also occur between unrelated vendors and in-house managers.
- The vendor selection process may be tampered with — leaking bid details from competitors to favored parties during the bidding process is common; we have even seen managers set up fake participants in vendor pitches to dupe their own purchasing department into believing that the business has been put up for a competitive bid.
- By paying inflated prices and/or not receiving the correct quantities of purchased goods, large sums can be siphoned off from a multinational company.

A couple of years ago, management at one of our companies decided to do a vendor review. In the process, we decided to change supplier for office materials. The existing vendor had been handled by the GM secretary and when she learned about the change of vendors she put in an unusually large order just before the switch. We called her in for an interview, and she immediately admitted to accepting kickbacks from the office materials supplier.

In this case, the scam would probably never have surfaced unless the employee had committed the error of placing that large order. But even so, it would have been easy to miss the indication that all was not right. How can we recognize corruption and what can we do about it? Here is what to do about corruption inside your own organization:

- *Assume that it goes on*: Vendors will actively solicit your colleagues with kickbacks — or come around at Chinese New Year, thanking them for their business over the year by presenting envelopes of money.
- *Be vigilant about positions of authority*: Purchasing, even for small items like air tickets or office supplies, can add up to significant sums. In marketing and other functions requiring the purchase of consulting services, it may be hard to judge vendors on "objective" criteria.
- *Have a clear written policy*: Try to forestall the constant temptations presented to your employees by external suppliers by having vendors sign a written policy (the signing is essential, verbal acceptance is not enough) stating clearly that any vendor providing kickbacks will be blacklisted. Make it clear to suppliers that "we do not want kickbacks, we want the lowest price".
- *Make sure you are a perfect role model*: Everything you do must be squeaky clean. Sony's Kawasaki notes that "it is exceedingly important to set a good example as a manager. I am meticulous about paying for minibars, private phone calls and other minor expenses. I must be seen as absolutely clean by my colleagues".
- *Manage all vendor selection as a group effort*: By involving several people from different functions in the choice of supplier, you greatly decrease the risk of any individual tampering with the purchasing process.
- *Handle business pitches confidentially*: Make sure that bids and proposals from different vendors are sealed and managed so as to prevent details being leaked to competitive vendors.

- *Introduce controls for suppliers*: You should include auditing rights and the right to conduct spot checks as part of your agreement with every supplier. This makes it easier to spot discrepancies in invoicing to your organization.
- *Watch out for long-standing supplier agreements — and sudden changes of supplier*: China is fiercely competitive and an unwillingness to change suppliers or failing to do a regular and transparent review is often a strong indicator that everything is not as it should. But if a long-standing supplier relationship is suddenly terminated without clear rationale, this could similarly be an indication that a cozy relationship has been upset, perhaps because a supplier refused to continue providing kickbacks.
- *Deal with anonymous letters*: Receiving an anonymous letter with serious allegations of malfeasance, perhaps against a well-like or trusted colleague, is not a pleasant experience, and managers anywhere may be tempted to simply throw such a letter away. But this is a common way of exposing fraud. "In my experience, the anonymous letter is the most common means whereby a fraud is exposed in a China business operation" says Peter Humphrey, the risk management consultant, who actually recommends proactively setting up an "ethics hotline or similar whistle blowing mechanism" to facilitate exposure of fraudulent practices.
- *Stay tuned in*: Nothing beats having your own, informal contacts at all levels of your organization. If you are well connected and in touch with your team, you will have a greater chance of being informed when there are rumors or suspicions.
- *Immediately fire any person who is discovered taking kickbacks*: If you know, you can assume that everybody knows; and if you do not do something about it, this knowledge will quickly demoralize your organization.

8.6.2. *Is guanxi a form of corruption?*

Although guanxi can certainly lead to corrupt practices, it must also be recognized as an important, and positive, force in

Chinese business and society. This adds another dimension of difficulty in identifying and dealing with corrupt practices. Should you ask employees to recommend friends and acquaintances to positions in your organization? How can you utilize the personal networks of colleagues in recommending excellent suppliers and vendors?

Our experience is that the contact networks are much too valuable to ignore. As long as processes are kept open and transparent, guanxi do not in themselves constitute corruption.

8.6.3. *What to do if you take over a corrupt organization*

As managers take over from predecessors, they change certain aspects of management. If you find yourself in charge of a joint venture or newly acquired subsidiary in China, unethical business practices will often be one area where you may have to deal with legacy problems. When you are new on the market, and do not have a "history" of paying bribes, establishing ethical practices is relatively easy. But what do you do if your customers are already used to getting kickbacks and your sales manager tells you all your competitors are doing the same thing? It takes a lot of skill, and courage, to clean up ingrained practices.

The first thing to do is to make sure you have top management support. On several occasions, Johan has taken on clients whose PR work in China had previously basically consisted of bribing journalists for writing positive articles. In such a situation, it is critical to hold an upfront discussion with the client about the short-term consequences of cutting off the pork: positive coverage tends to go down sharply and individual journalists, upset about losing a steady source of income, may write critical articles about the company out of spite. Long-term, we have proved a professional and ethical way of working to be more effective in generating positive coverage, but the short-term effects are always there. If the client is presented with the consequences, beforehand and in a clear way, you have your back free to effect the necessary changes. Similarly, your first move as a manager should be to present the situation to your superiors and suggest a way to clean up your act. Management will often be worried that "China is different" and so may be reluctant to accept your advice. You need to present them with clear arguments for why the status quo is not acceptable.

You may also want to proceed gradually. Instead of cutting off the unethical practice in one fell swoop, it is often more practical to formulate ethical policies against certain deadlines. For example, when Anders recently took over an existing organization where kickbacks to customers were prevalent, he set up individual meetings with sales managers to communicate the imminent change in policy. Reactions were mixed, but not all negative — one of the local managers even responded that "this is great because now I can rely on an official policy which disallows bribes, and this will make negotiations easier for me". More reluctant managers were informed that "The money will be approved for those deals that have already been signed, but starting from next time, we are prohibiting this behavior". The response was surprisingly moderated, and we did not lose any customers. Some customers actually expressed appreciation for the changed policy. Perhaps they were happy to be rid of internal discussions about how to split the money?

8.6.4. *Company chops*

Company "chops" or stamps are such an important part of local business — but also such a common instrument of misdemeanor — that they require some detailed discussion. In China, chops replace or complement individual signatures on most legal documents, checks, etc. Chops, often intricately carved and beautifully executed, come in many guises. There are several different kinds of corporate chops for different uses, as well as personal chops for individuals. A signed contract will be deemed invalid unless it has been chopped with the appropriate seals — even the signature of the company's General Manager will not be accepted without the company chop to accompany it.

Conversely, a chop will suffice, without any signature, to sign binding agreements, form corporate entities or take loans in the name of the company. With the company chop in hand, a local manager has the equivalent of a wide-ranging affidavit to do almost anything on behalf of the company.

The use of chops has direct consequences for the workings of the Chinese legal system, and therefore on the structuring of Western companies. Chinese law requires the signature of the "legal person" of the mother company for certain changes to the registration of a subsidiary. Let us say that a Fortune-500 company registers a company in China as a subsidiary of global head office. This would mean that the Chairman of the Board of the worldwide company would need to put his personal signature on a change of General Manager for the Chinese company or some equally mundane matter. In China, this would be solved by the appropriate Officer of the company being entrusted with the use of the Chairman's seal — something which would render any Western CFO a nervous wreck. To avoid causing later problems, a Western company investing or acquiring a company in China actually needs to use an investment vehicle where the legal person will be available to sign the necessary documents.

The chop system is so alien to Western practices that the typical CFO of a multinational will simply say "this can't be true!" But you ignore the implications at your peril. There must be clear policies in place, and chops must be carefully stored and handled to prevent malfeasance. Some basic features of a good chop policy are:

- *That it is written down*: Detailing how chops are used and stored. Peter Humphrey comments that "considering how difficult it is for expatriate managers to understand the significance of chops, having a written policy and process for usage are absolutely crucial".
- *Checks and balances*: No single individual must have the control of any company chop. This includes the General Manager of the company.

- *Separate the physical possession and right to use*: The custodian's role should be just that — keeping the chops and signing them out for predefined purposes, or, in case of doubt, to gain approval from a more senior manager before handing out the chop.
- *If you want an enforceable document, get it chopped*: The flip side of keeping track of your own chops is that you must ensure that the other party chops any legal document. Just getting the General Manager's signature is not enough — without the company chop, a Chinese company can simply claim ignorance of a document; this becomes especially easy if the signatory person is no longer employed.

8.7. Culture and Corporate Brand

The prestige of working for a "famous company" is a major competitive advantage for multinationals in China. Customers really do care about the company behind the products they buy — even a company like Procter & Gamble, famous for focusing its worldwide communications efforts on individual product brands, adopted a strategy of always promoting the corporate logo in its Chinese TV commercials. We will discuss brand-building from a marketing perspective later in the book. But brand image and corporate culture are closely interrelated — given the importance of face in China, the reputation of your company will be just as important to existing and potential employees as it is to your customers. Chinese coworkers like to work for well known and respected companies. The advantage of market leadership is therefore even more manifest in China than in Western countries. As an entrepreneurial upstart, Eastwei had much greater problems attracting senior recruits from competitors than would have been the case in a Western market. As the company grew a leading reputation, it rapidly became easier to lure consultants over from well-known multinational agencies.

Major multinationals invest heavily in so-called Corporate Social Responsibility programs in China. These often take the form of charity donations, sponsorships, or cooperation projects with Chinese government institutions. Still, it is striking how opportunistic and reactive most such efforts have been — companies tend to involve themselves in CSR programs because the "Chinese government", whatever that means in this context, is supposedly concerned with seeing a "commitment to China".

While most major multinationals have been working actively with marketing communications in China for a long time, they have only recently woken up to the importance of a coherent strategy for building a sharp corporate image on the local market. Such a strategy needs to take into account the following factors:

- Who is the target group? A strong corporate image serves to reassure customers of the quality of products, but for B2B companies the more important target group may actually be local employees.
- What do you want your company to be known for in China? How will you meet the needs of your target groups, be they customers or potential recruits? This is about more than just being seen as a "good corporate citizen" in general.
- Which are your strengths compared to the competition? How can you reinforce these to provide even greater competitive advantages?
- External branding is only one side of the coin. For some companies, for example in the telecommunications and luxury goods industries, China has already become the largest market in the world. For the majority, China is still a relatively small market, but even so, many multinationals have extensive production operations in the country. Companies now have thousands, even tens of thousands, of employees in China. This poses new challenges for employee or "internal" communications. These challenges are especially important for companies that are also growing rapidly. Many multinationals are now putting in place sophisticated internal

communications programs on a par with those implemented at head office.

8.8. Security

Corruption is not the only security challenge for companies in China. But corruption exacerbates worldwide security issues in addition to creating China-specific problems.

For most business people today, weak management of data and information are the most burning issue. Because of corruption and personal guanxi, business people must assume that competitors can lay their hands on all kinds of communications and data, be they letter, faxes, e-mails, or mobile phone messages, that the authorities are warehousing for future use. Companies would be naive to assume that competitors do not have access to patent applications, encryption systems for telecommunications, and other proprietary technologies. With the right connections, anyone can get hold of data from leaky government bodies.

Peter Humphrey, the risk management expert, emphasizes that most security problems do not emanate from "James Bond-style technical eavesdropping". However, in sensitive industries such as automobiles, aircraft, satellites, life sciences, and nanotechnology, there is a "lively trade" in confidential information — an employee may be bribed to provide intelligence, or tricked by an ostensible headhunter into providing sensitive facts in an interview situation. There have also been instances of state-owned enterprises or even government agencies enticing employees of multinationals to provide trade secrets to support domestic businesses.

Information security becomes especially problematic in JV situations, where employees may retain strong loyalties to the local partner. But even in wholly owned companies, managers should implement best practices in data protection and be aware of the high risk of IPR thefts. Prudent business people stay aware of these problems and limit the access to, and communication of, sensitive information accordingly.

8.9. IPR Protection

In the mid-1990s, Johan started a music record company that licensed Western music to the Chinese market. Over four years' time, he secured some 30 CD's, including world-famous artists like British synth band Depeche Mode as well as the first officially sanctioned hard rock and heavy metal releases in China. At one time, Johan discovered that a popular dance compilation on sale around Beijing contained two dance tracks from one of his licensed artists. A quick market survey in the form of calls to major music stores around the country suggested that the compilation had sold around 200,000 copies, which meant that he had been cheated out of some 40,000 RMB based on the going royalty standard per song in the industry. The compilation had been put out by a state-owned record company. When Johan contacted them, a flustered VP promised that someone would call back "within an hour". Fifteen minutes later, an out-of-town businessman called: "I understand the problem, don't do anything rash, let's meet for lunch in Beijing next Monday, OK?" After an amiable lunch conversation, where the flown-in business counterpart studiously avoided discussing anything relating to music, Johan finally brought up "our little copyright problem". "Yes, I understand that you want to get paid for the use of your songs", said the businessman, opening an attaché case on top of the remains of our lunch. "Will this be enough?" Inside the case were four bundles of one hundred 100-RMB notes, exactly the sum I had surmised he owed us. "That will do nicely", I said, and picked up the money. I kept the case as well.

Johan's record company can serve as an illustration of Chinese IPR issues in general. On the regulatory side, the authorities actually unwittingly abetted the pirates. Because the Chinese government retains ultimate control of culture — books, movies, and music recordings — a legal record release was an onerous affair. It entailed first finding a Chinese distribution partner willing to release the record locally. One would then buy a license for each record from a state-owned music publisher, since only approved companies were allowed to release music — such trading in licenses was technically not allowed, but had become the established industry practice. Once the license had been acquired, all lyrics had to be submitted to the censors. The approval process typically took more than one month. By that time, any record with serious potential would already be available on the market in not just one, but several pirated versions. The irony of this, of course, is that the authorities ended up clamping down on the legitimate business, which at the time accounted for less than 5% of the total, while having no control of the 95% supplied by the pirates. The government ended up losing even the potential tax revenues while maintaining "control" only in name over what Chinese kids could listen to. But the story of the pirated dance tracks also illustrates a bigger issue: the importance of having an IPR strategy and promptly and actively following up on any infractions.

IPR infringement in China is more than a legal issue — it is a complex mixture of, on the one hand, deliberate malfeasance, ignorance, and opportunism by business people; and, on the other, misdirected efforts at management, corruption, and lack of capacity for enforcement.

Loosely, there are two types of IPR violator: The real pirates are underground syndicates who deliberately copy software, music and products in order to flog them as the real thing, or at least a replacement for it. But there is also an opportunistic form of piracy where a legitimate company, or an adventurous individual (which can, of course, be the CEO) at a legitimate company copies products or uses IP in an inappropriate way, in the simple hope that nobody will notice. Often, no-one does.

When faced with the rampant IPR violations in China, Western managers may draw the wrong conclusions: "If we are going to get pirated anyways, let's just accept this as a cost of doing business in

China. What's the use of spending money, time and effort in trying to prevent the inevitable?" China has a modern legal and regulatory framework; corporate law is largely built on the US model. Implementation is still patchy, but if companies apply best practices in protecting their IPR under Chinese law, they run a much better chance of success in stemming all but the most cunning infringements. Lawyer Fraser Mendel provides some good advice:

- *Register all your IPR*: Protection for patents and trademarks may not be as easy to enforce as in your home market, but if you do not register them in China, chances are that somebody else will — and then sue *you* for infringement. Although lack of enforcement may not allow you to use your trademark offensively, you still need to register it for defensive purposes.
- *Make sure your lawyers understand the regulatory regime*: Transferring trademarks and technology into China, for example, requires registration with the authorities. Without such registration, trademark and patent protection is not enforceable under Chinese law. One major multinational recently discovered that failure to register trademarks that it had licensed to Chinese companies rendered it without any legal recourse when its Chinese customers simply refused to pay the several million US dollars they owed. In fact, Chinese law does not permit royalty payments abroad if the trademark has not been registered in China, and unscrupulous local companies have been known to actively use this loophole to "test the market" and then simply refusing to pay royalties if the business did not prove attractive enough to continue.
- *Control your local employees*: Apply best practices in IPR protection by including nondisclosure clauses in employment contracts, restricting access to sensitive material, etc.
- *Make your organization aware of the issue*: The frontline sales and after-sales people will often be the first to be aware of violations — make sure they understand the importance of actually reporting to management when they hear from a

customer that "hey, I had someone trying to sell me an almost identical product at a cheaper price last week".

- *Show that you care*: Johan received his missing royalties because he was prepared to actively enforce his rights. Copyright infringers may mend their ways if they are caught with their fingers in the cookie jar — or at least if someone actively starts to seek redress for their violations. The easiest way to do this is through "administrative action", for example a raid by the relevant government agency. Companies seeking redress will need to prove that infringement has taken place, as well as showing that they have made the appropriate registrations to protect their IPR. You may also have to pay for the enforcement action upfront.

Mendel also points out the two most common problems with contracts in China: making sure that disputes should be handled by binding arbitration, and that they are enforceable.

Chapter 9

Right Business Focus

As we have seen, there are many examples of how international business people overestimate the Chinese market potential for their products. As the economy develops and matures, and experience and market data become more readily available, this may be changing. But even so, or perhaps precisely because the market is developing so rapidly, a sharp focus becomes even more important. We have seen managers fail because they were "forever chasing the potential" — there always seemed to be a bigger pot of gold around the corner in China. China is a huge country with a rapidly growing economy. This is great news for business, but it also carries a big danger: loss of focus. There are several reasons why maintaining both business and geographical focus in China is so important:

- Clear business focus drives a strong corporate culture.
- China's size and the lack of maturity in some industries makes it easy to spread efforts too thinly; the opportunities are so many that choosing the right ones becomes an issue.
- Chinese customers often need to be managed more closely, both in order to provide the right level of service, and to ensure a healthy business relationship, timely payments, etc.
- The rapidly changing market often results in inconsistent implementation of strategy.
- Distribution and other bottlenecks may prevent companies from addressing some geographies or market segments.

Let us see look at each of these issues in turn to see how we can avoid repeating the worst mistakes.

9.1. Clear Business Focus Drives a Strong Corporate Culture

We have already discussed the importance of actively building a strong corporate culture in China. In a market environment where opportunities often abound while human resources are scarce and where you are often competing for the best talent rather than for the business as such, a clear business focus sends a strong signal to existing and prospective employees: "This company is expert and focused, and will provide ample opportunity for me to develop as a professional". Sticking to a razor-sharp business focus makes it easier for a rapidly growing organization to maintain momentum.

9.2. Market Size and Maturity

China is not only a large country — it is also complex and highly segmented. Even a country which is comparable in size, such as the USA, is vastly more developed when it comes to infrastructure and logistics, and probably more homogeneous when it comes to customer tastes and preferences as well. Few, if any, countries provide as bewildering an array of opportunities as China.

Strategy will usually need to be localized for every province, even every city. This is especially true for consumer products, but even preferences for some industrial products show large differences between different regions. You will need to understand local market preferences, set up local distribution deals, perhaps even establish offices in the most promising markets. Understanding where those markets are, picking the low-hanging fruit, as it were, requires that you concentrate your efforts from the very outset.

Another reason for caution and focus in pursuing business opportunities is the low level of development of some industries in China. There may simply be no need for your product in some regions. And even when there is an opportunity, are you sure that this will lead you to a sustainable business? When a particular market is wide open, it is tempting to pursue every segment where you have a product, but the mere fact that your local competitors are not very active yet does not mean they will not be. You should choose to enter defensible market segments where you have a long-term chance of staying competitive as the market develops.

9.3. Speed of Change — Peter's Story

While every business person in China must be prepared to take opportunities on the run in the fast-moving local market, the fluid nature of the business environment requires you to have a clear picture of which opportunities to pursue and which ones to let go.

Let us look at an example of how confusing this complex and rapidly changing environment can be to managers from other, more mature markets. Peter, a product line sales manager with a few years of sales experience from abroad, had been newly appointed to a China position at a large company that Anders worked with. As Peter came to China to take up his new job, he was presented with a number of interesting prospects, and immediately started to approach them for business. The initial feedback was good — the Chinese customers showed strong interest and discussions continued. But it proved harder than expected to close any deals. After a few weeks of negotiations, Peter gradually lost interest — especially since he had, in the meantime, found some larger, even more interesting customer. After a couple of months of "chasing the potential", Peter sat down with Anders to analyze the situation. At this time, he was frustrated and disappointed — an ambitious young sales manager trying to do the right things for the company and becoming increasingly fed up with the Chinese reality.

After a couple of discussion sessions, Peter and Anders agreed that the lessons learned were valuable ones. The time had not been wasted — since there was a lack of reliable market data, homework and "learning by doing" would be an important part of Peter's strategy going forward. It was also agreed, however, that the long-term solution to the problem would be better intelligence ground work, careful priorities, and perseverance. The way forward would be to carefully define target segments, focus on the most important targets, and stick with them until clear results were seen.

First of all, we looked at the overall market situation. Since, as is typical in China, all of the company's major international competitors were present on the market, it turned out that competition for the largest customers was severe and that prices and profitability were suffering as a result. Instead, we identified an opportunity to develop relationships with smaller, but growing, customers.

As in so many other cases, the mere size of China was another problem. Over the last decades, China has made enormous investments in infrastructure. Transport by air works as well as anywhere else. The motorway network has also become quite extensive, which means that road transportation is turning into the preferred mode of transport. Even though railways are still slow, speed has increased in recent years. The arrival of good international logistics companies has also helped distribution of products and will do so even more in the future.

In short, these recent improvements to the distribution infrastructure allowed us to reach customers all over the country. Many of the potential customers we had identified were located outside our traditional markets in Beijing, Shanghai, and Guangzhou. We needed to prioritize those areas where we could find efficient distribution solutions.

Another important component of the sales strategy was to identify the customers with the greatest potential for growth. This becomes especially important in a growth market like China's — companies that outpace the already high average growth figures in your industry are often more profitable and liquid, and can therefore contribute significantly to your company's bottom line. Identifying growing customers allows you to "grow with the customer", the least expensive way to increase sales. This opportunity is especially attractive in a fast-growing market like China.

As a result of the new strategy, Peter built a solid high-growth business with good profit margins. Armed with the experience and sales team from this success, he later also successfully broke into some of the larger, more centrally located customers, albeit still with lower margins than the small-customer business.

Peter is not an isolated case, and neither is the problem limited to expatriate managers in China. An oft-repeated (although not entirely accurate) management saw claims "the Chinese character for 'crisis' or 'danger' is the same as the one for 'opportunity'". The saying is usually used as "proof" that adversity often brings with it new opportunities, but it applies just as well to the opposite claim: too much opportunity can, in itself, be dangerous. This "opportunity problem" requires constant management attention. Anders could not help but suppress a happy smile when he heard Peter tell his local managers at a sales meeting, a year after his arrival, that "it is better to do a few things right, and stick with them, than to constantly jump from one opportunity to another".

9.4. Distribution is a Major Bottleneck

In the previous section, we alluded to the fact that it may be difficult to address certain geographical segments in the Chinese market simply due to logistics and distribution problems. For years, distribution was off-limits to multinational companies. The situation was compounded by local protectionism in the form of unofficial purchasing preferences, lacking infrastructure and of course bona fide competition from locally entrenched companies. Sometimes, even the passage of provincial borders can be a problem, as local police harass out-of-province truck drivers with speeding tickets and other burdens.

In order to address this problem, China has recently relaxed limitations on foreign investments in logistics, transports, and warehousing. The central government has also spent huge amounts of money on infrastructure investments, which are seen as a way of spreading the wealth from the coastal provinces inland to the country's western regions.

A few years ago it was almost impossible to find world-class distributors in China. There were basically two options available:

- SOEs, government institutions, or research institutes, all of which moved into distribution as a complement to existing business or a way of survival in the face of market challenges and budget cuts.
- Entrepreneurial individuals, who saw an opportunity to make quick money and who were not really interested in, or had the time, to build up a long-term relationship neither with you as the supplier or with the customers.

Neither of these options were prone to produce forward-thinking partners with a long-term commitment leveraging each party's unique strength in a mutually advantageous and sustainable business relationship. But while the remnants of the planned economy seldom did well in the market, some of the private entrepreneurs have now built excellent organizations that combine the best of Chinese business acumen with internationally recognized business practices.

Today it is therefore much easier to find a distributor than what used to be the case. Still, distribution remains such a major challenge that it needs to be a carefully considered part of any business plan for China. It also needs to be an integral element of the due diligence process for any investment or marketing plan.

Some of the aspects of distribution to consider as you consider distribution in your business plan are:

- *Partners*: Choosing the right one can make or break your business. As outlined in the section on finding business partners, the key is to spread your net widely to make sure you have really trawled through all the available choices of distributor or agent.
- *Distribution agreements*: Do not assume that the distributor will deliver on oral promises. Always set minimum sales quotas

and leave provisions for regularly reviewing, with the possibility of terminating, every distribution deal.

- *Do regional deals*: China is huge, and most distributors will be stronger in some areas than in others. They may accept taking a regional rather than national distribution deal. In some cases, it also makes sense to structure distribution by industry.

- *Demand exclusivity*: Given the complexity and immaturity of the Chinese market, having distributors representing your competitors is asking for trouble. Avoid this wherever possible by demanding exclusivity of your agents.

- *Do not overestimate the management savvy of the agent*: Make sure that commissions and other rewards are carefully designed to reward the right behaviors, and if possible try to influence how the agent rewards his own sales people.

- *Provide the right support*: Some of the best and most entrepreneurial local distributors have grown from small operations based on strong guanxi networks of the founders. As a multinational with worldwide experience from your industry, your company can provide tremendous value to these distributors by providing education in everything from technical know-how to salesmanship and marketing. At Sandvik, Anders built a distribution network that outsold any competitor by providing extensive training in return for exclusivity.

- *Maintain high-touch*: As in all business dealings in China, face time will allow you to build trusted relationships. Regular meetings to discuss and agree on business plans are essential in making sure that the distributor's organization, rather than just the owner, understands and buys into your distribution strategy.

Chapter 10
Support Your Frontline Sales Organization

The old saying that you "are either employed as a salesperson or as somebody who supports the salesperson" holds especially true in the intensely competitive Chinese marketplace. The sales function is so important, and so challenging, in China that it warrants its very own focus: Supporting what we call the "frontline", i.e. the sales reps and promoters who are in direct contact with the end customer and actually drive our business. These people are a key but oft-neglected asset in China. Every company succeeds or fails in the critical meeting between its sales force and its Chinese customers.

Multinationals have faced difficult, even insurmountable challenges in cracking the local market. In view of these problematic experiences, there are analysts who feel that most companies would be better off just leaving the Chinese marketplace alone and focusing on production for re-export. Before talking about how to build and motivate a sales force in China, it therefore seems appropriate to discuss whether or not we should be building a sales force in the first place.

10.1. Production With or Without Local Sales?

As we have argued, the Chinese marketplace may be the most cluttered and competitive in the world — everyone wants to get a piece of the pie, so you will find yourself competing against Americans, Europeans, Japanese, Koreans and a plethora of local companies, some of which will be state subsidized or belong to government institutions that also function as regulators. Some markets are partially off-limits to foreign companies and protectionism in the provinces can skew the purchasing decisions of local buyers, especially for business-to-business products. Still, there are some compelling reasons for establishing a sales organization on the ground in China.

The most straightforward reason is of course that most companies actually do manage to sell successfully in China. In some categories, this already *is* the world's largest market, and a market that can be profitably exploited. If your sales organization is built well and prudently managed, China will usually become a profitable market for your company.

Another consideration is more strategic: the risk for complacency. In our experience, some of the companies who use China as a production and supply base for export will over time find themselves facing new challenges by not selling in China. Since production costs are low, there is a risk that the China operations do not become as efficient as they could be because they are (at least for the time being) "efficient enough" when they sell to high-cost and high-price markets abroad. It may therefore be wise to directly expose oneself to the local Chinese price levels, and thus continuously measure oneself against the local competition. Sooner or later, you will face the "China price" from competitors on your home or export markets anyway.

It often makes most sense to start by importing products, gradually building a local sales organization, and then starting local production once the sales network has already been established. Such "import-first" strategies allow for greater focus and usually provides an opportunity to establish a higher price profile, which can later be exploited for locally manufactured products.

In any case, most multinational companies sooner or later choose to build a sales organization in China. This is by no means easy.

10.2. Establishing a Sales Organization

Whether your customers are housewives or corporate purchasing departments, your sales force are the people who will be in daily contact with them. These interactions have been called the "moments of truth" for the organization, because they determine more than just each particular sale — they influence pricing, brand image, and the ability to quickly adapt to changing market conditions. It is this frontline activity that drives revenue and pays for all other corporate functions. If you have decided to enter the Chinese marketplace, the quality of your sales team will be *the* determining factor of your success.

But there are also other reasons that make the sales force a key issue:

- China's large size is especially problematic if one compares it with the actual dollar size of the market — one could say that the potential of China's market is huge but "diluted" over a vast territory. To cover all of China is currently impossible; in order to have a serious presence in the majority of cities with populations larger than, say, half a million or even a million, a typical provider of household products may need to cover more than a hundred cities and employ several thousand promoters reporting to sales managers numbering in the hundreds. But even B2B suppliers will need to have a large sales force. By 2004, Sandvik had more than 200 sales people in nearly 20 offices — to cover what we estimated to be 60% of the Chinese market for our products.
- Chinese companies have a tradition of selling on price. Sales people, particularly those with a background in local companies, will go to great lengths to persuade you that a high-price strategy is not suited to the Chinese reality, where, so the story goes, "the only thing that matters is price". Motivating your sales team to sell on value is a long-term, high-touch education effort.
- Even if you do sell at a good price, getting paid is often a problem. In B2B industrial sales, sales people need to be responsible

for collecting payments — they need to have the self-confidence and skills to challenge tardy or recalcitrant payers.

- Corruption within the own organization can put severe pressure on prices. When your sales representatives boost their income through price collusion with customers — "I give you a 10% discount, if you give me half of the money" — your bottom line suffers. Although we deal with general problems of kickbacks and corruption elsewhere in the book, this problem is especially intractable in the context of sales.

In a mature organization with a lot of accumulated drive and experience, the sales force tends to take on its own momentum — continue providing your sales team with great products at competitive prices and sales will take care of themselves. It is therefore easy for a China manager coming out of the parent company to forget the important role of the frontline sales people. In his or her experience, it is enough to get busy with what he/she may regard as more important matters while the sales persons go on doing their thing. But on the Chinese market, the sales force will require your direct and unwavering attention.

Most foreign enterprises are relatively new to China, so we often do not have the luxury of a mature organization to fall back on. The sales force is no exception. When we do have a mature organization is China, it is often because we have taken over or formed a joint venture with a Chinese company. In that type of organization, there can be severe problems with the sales force. These problems are often more complicated than simple lack of experience. We have dealt with these extensively in the more general context of managing a joint venture.

Before the WTO agreement came into effect, only those foreign companies which had established production in China were allowed to sell directly to end customers. They were, strictly speaking, only legally allowed to sell the products that had actually been produced in China, although some of them worked around these rules by using Chinese intermediaries or agents. The limitations on sales organizations led multinational companies to put too much management time and focus into building and setting up of the production, leaving too little energy for building up the sales force. This would have been alright for companies focusing exclusively on production for export, but in fact the vast majority of multinational companies came to China with an eye to the local market. Failure to focus on the frontline sales organization has doomed some foreign companies in China. Sales and production must be built up in parallel and receive the right amount of attention. Getting this right at the outset is much easier than fixing potential problems at a later stage. If your own background is in production or engineering, you need to be especially mindful of the sales challenge.

This challenge starts with recruitment.

10.3. Recruiting Frontline Sales People

What kind of people can and should I find for my sales team? China is a human-resource scarce country; experienced sales people, especially sales managers, are in high demand. If you also require English skills, the search becomes harder by a power of two. The first questions to ask are therefore:

- Do I really need older people with industry and/or sales experience?
- Or should I employ young and relatively inexperienced people that are more malleable?

There are obviously advantages and disadvantages to both approaches. Older people have more experience. This experience will certainly provide a quicker start to the sales effort compared with what younger, less experienced people can provide. On the other hand, there is a risk that "experience" has produced undesirable side effects: work or managements style which does not fit your organization, or unethical practices that conflict with the way your company does business. It is often difficult for a sales person who is used to selling in a certain way (for example, paying kickbacks to customers) to change his or her ways. Instead, such a person may spend energy trying to change the company, failing which he or she will leave.

By "young people" we mean university-educated individuals, preferably in their second job after graduation. Taking people directly from university can sometimes work, but in China a modicum of working experience is usually preferable. One reason for this is the Chinese emphasis on interpersonal relations; it usually takes a year or two for a fresh graduate to gain some initial maturity in handling workplace and customer relations. Another reason is team stability; research published regularly by the big human resources consulting firms in China consistently shows that fresh graduates tend to leave their first job rather quickly, often within a year or two, but are more stable in their second job.

Young people are easier to shape and they can more readily be trained to sell in the way your company wants them to. The relative lack of experience means that it will take a longer time before they reach the same sales figures that the more experienced sales people can produce.

The "right" approach therefore depends on your situation. If your sales effort is heavily dependent on in-depth industry knowledge or relationships that can only be built over the long term, you may opt for key competitive hires of senior talent in order to kickstart your organization — but again, be aware that the importance of guanxi or relationships is often exaggerated by your local organization. If you do opt for experienced talent, be aware of the potential challenges and make sure that you have the management bandwidth to ensure that the team will work in the way you want them to. Managing a mature team will require you to pay special attention to:

- *Forcing teamwork*: Tie appraisals and bonuses to delivery of not just sales results, but also meticulous input of customers and sales leads into a shared sales database. Experienced sales people are notoriously territorial and will sometimes keep their customer contacts "secret" from the rest of the organization.

They will typically keep their name card collections locked in their top drawers, taking them along if they move on to your competitors.

- *Preventing corruption*: Put in place checks and balances to prevent unsavory practices. If sales people feel that there are sophisticated financial and other controls in place, they will feel less tempted to complement their income or achieve "easy sales" through commissions. On a more positive note, providing hands-on support for your frontline people will show that you care and that you have your eye on the organizations successes as well as failures.

If you need to build a large sales force and have the luxury of planning and time, go for younger, more malleable recruits. In this case, you should:

- *Hire for attitude*: For a salesperson, educational background may be important — but the individual's attitude is incomparably more so. A sales person's character is the most important factor determining his or her success in selling. It is often easier to judge the character and attitude of young people. If you do not feel you would buy from this guy, do not hire him!
- *Avoid disqualifying women*: Women are often successful even in traditionally "male" positions in China.
- *Hire for potential*: Hire for talent and potential rather than for skills and experience. Young Chinese professionals are ambitious and learn fast — you may be surprised by just how quickly they develop. If you can develop a "first generation" of sales people steeped in the ways and culture of your company, they will form a solid foundation for rapid expansion of the sales force. It is also easier to find young English-speaking sales people without compromising on personality and other talents.

As we have seen in a more general perspective, when it comes to promoting younger, less experienced colleagues, you need to provide leadership, role modeling and mentoring and provide extensive training. Otherwise, you risk filling the knowledge gap with the very sales practices you avoided by hiring inexperienced people in the first place.

10.4. Training, Developing, and Retaining Sales People

Making the right choice of candidate is the obvious first step in creating a strong field sales force. But as we have seen, once you have great people on board, your challenge in China will be to keep them. Nowhere is this challenge greater than in the sales team, where the results can be clearly measured and bonus and commission systems keep employees focused on their own bottom line as well as the company's. Through training and development, you can ensure that sales people and other employees stay and continue to contribute to the development of your operations.

Sales people are so interested in getting access to training that they will often sacrifice weekends or evenings. This can help solve the problem of taking the sales force away from customers for the duration of a training session.

The observations above are, as we have seen, valid for the organization as a whole, but especially for the sales force. They are the "loneliest" people in any organization — when they face the customer, they only have themselves to rely on. But there are also training needs that are specific to China and to the sales function:

- *Benefit-driven sales*: Chinese sales people, particularly in B2B sectors, tend to have engineering backgrounds and often focus the sales effort on specifications rather than customer benefits. Teaching sales people to take a larger perspective and seeing the customer's business from the customer's point of view, is motivating and can yield excellent results. At Sandvik, we successfully trained the sales force in analyzing and selling in productivity benefits that the customer could reap by using our cutting tools. Johan has worked with training on selling in end-user benefits, rather than technical specifications, for a number of large consumer goods companies. The importance of this type of training will remain barring major changes to the Chinese schooling system.

- *Understanding customer psychology and organization*: In any market, using rational arguments to sell the product is not enough — we must also understand the customer's need to justify a particular purchase to his own colleagues. Chinese customer organizations are often hierarchical, and the overall business climate makes it important for the individual responsible for a purchase to present compelling arguments, especially when buying from a new supplier. We have seen that Chinese coworkers are reluctant to stick their necks out and take responsibility for important decisions; a buyer will therefore most likely try to confirm his choice of supplier with a higher-ranking decision maker in the company. If you are selling a premium product, which is more costly than that of the competition, your customer's requirement for good arguments becomes even stronger in order to allay potential suspicions of self-interest or foul play in making the more expensive choice. Training sales personnel in this psychology and how to provide compelling arguments for the customer to take back to his boss can reap handsome rewards.

- *Teamwork*: The problems with teamwork are not only limited to hoarding of information or other turf-defending behavior. The tendency of Chinese sales people to be individual heroes means that they sometimes act counterproductively by failing to leverage the power of the own organization — psychologically as well as in practice. For example, a sales person may be reluctant to bring in engineering support until after the sale is made — even in cases where it would seem that the engineer could clearly have been useful in persuading the customer. Training consultant Per Dahl points out that in training sessions, Chinese colleagues tend to evaluate their own teamwork skills more favorably than their managers do.

- *Handling concrete market problems*: Training should take into account the realities of the Chinese market. Local sales people should be given concrete skills to handle specific challenges, for example requests for kickbacks. Per Dahl points out another reason for the need to make training China-relevant: "Chinese colleagues are extremely receptive to training, but some programs are rejected because trainees do not feel that contents are relevant to China. The trainer must convince trainees that he or she understands the Chinese reality. This can be done by initially focusing on cultural differences such as giving face, hierarchical and authoritarian organizations and so on. Only after these idiosyncrasies have been acknowledged will local colleagues accept experiences which are more universally valid".

In Sandvik, we used a concept that we called Senior Sales people. We found that in mature markets outside China, we often had experienced older sales people, who were not being used in the most effective way but could provide a great deal of value in China. A typical example were older sales people who had been promoted to managerial positions thanks to outstanding sales records. Candidates were often nearing retirement and were not always happy about having been "promoted away" from sales, which had been the area in which they had been at their very best.

These Senior Sales people would spend about one month at a time in China, usually 4–5 times per year. Their task was to be out on the field with our junior sales people, meeting customers and actively developing the market — according to an informal rule, they were not "allowed" to spend time at the office. This allowed them to become great hands-on role models for the younger people in our Chinese organization. The effects were fantastic. Everybody came out as a winner: The subsidiary abroad where the Senior Sales person normally worked, could make organizational changes and increase efficiency. The Senior Sales person himself was allowed to work with what they were good at and loved doing: real selling. Our young local sales people developed rapidly with the help of these experienced mentors. But we also found that there were a few crucial considerations to make:

- *Choice of mentors*: Since the Senior Sales person tended to have a large influence on the fledgling local coworker, the choice of mentors for the program was critical. We spent a lot of time identifying and interviewing these people, but we were surprised at how many we could locate at our various overseas subsidiaries.
- *Time limits*: Using 4–5 one-month mentorship periods spread out over the year prevented the mentors from stifling the independence and creativity of the local juniors. It is important that the Senior Sales person only function as a complement to the local organization and does not take authority away from the local sales person's manager.

We also identified a few opportunities where the Senior Sales persons could provide truly unique benefits to the local organization. For example, systematically using the Senior Sales persons as door openers to foreign companies of the same nationality as the Senior Sales person himself proved to be a particularly successful application of the program.

10.5. Point-of-Sales Promoters

A typical consumer-goods company will employ thousands of sales people at point of sales in retail outlets across China. The point-of-sales promoters are often under utilized. They have relatively low pay, surviving on commissions. They tend to have a low level of education. They are lonely, in the sense that they often left to their own devices in far-flung locations and not under the direct daily influence of your company. Visit a Chinese retail outlet, and you will often find promoters covering for each other, in essence representing several brands at once even though they are paid by a particular company.

The key point to make about sales promoters in China is that it is not just enough to motivate them through sales bonuses. A bonus influences your behavior only if you know how to improve your chances of receiving it — if you are not skilled in sales techniques, do not know your products and do not understand the company you are selling for, the bonus becomes a variable part of your paycheck, nothing more.

Successful companies in China invest a lot in promoter training. You can also use simple but effective internal marketing tools to make sure that sales promoters are bang up-to-date on new product benefits and company developments. A few straightforward examples would include:

- *DVD instruction disks*: Provide information in a more direct and intuitive way than written manuals on new products. Disks can include a discussion of TV commercials and instructions on how to leverage particular consumer benefits at point of sales.
- *Interesting media articles about your offering*: Articles from reputable papers and magazines are easy to digest and offer third-party endorsement and credibility which is hard to duplicate using brochures and other corporate material.
- *Online multiple-choice tests*: Ensure that promoters have watched, read, and understood critical materials. Can be tied to bonus schemes.

Such tools are inexpensive to produce but can make a huge difference in the meeting with customers.

10.6. Motivating the Sales Organization

Training, we believe, is a great motivator. What other ways can we use to stimulate a sales organization in China? The most obvious motivation tool is the incentive or sales bonus scheme employed. In our experience, a bonus scheme is useful, but not strictly necessary. Its main benefit is allowing sales people to receive high compensation without influencing the overall pay structure of your organization. If you do implement a bonus program, however, it must be carefully designed so that it becomes not only "extra pay", but also drives the kind of behavior that the company wants. Chinese colleagues will, to an even higher degree than Westerners we have worked with, analyze the system and optimize it to their own benefit. Using "straight commissions" is therefore a sure way of motivating "sales at any cost" behavior, without regard for long-term considerations such as whether customers can actually pay.

We have already discussed the importance of maintaining a clear business focus in China. This is especially relevant in a B2B sales context; the sales effort should be expanded in stages as solid bridgeheads are built in various areas. A clear focus will also act as a strong motivator. The more you limit a sales person's choice — geographically, by industry, type of customer and so on — the better the results will often be.

The commission system should therefore be tailored to provide incentives for all types of desirable behavior:

- raising prices
- developing new customers of the "right" kind
- introduction of new products or services
- sharing of sales information and other business intelligence into a collective database
- collection of debts.

Because of the common difficulties in collecting accounts receivables, any sales commission system in China should be based on "money collected" rather than "sales made". Getting paid is actually such an important business challenge that it deserves a special strategy of its own.

10.7. Getting Paid

From time to time, international media will discuss the large amounts of bad loans burdening the Chinese banks and the problem of outstanding accounts receivable between Chinese corporations. Large local enterprises have had such serious cash-flow problems that they have not been able to pay salaries or welfare benefits for months at a time. There is no reliable credit rating system in China. As we have seen, it can even be difficult to find any financial information at all about a prospective customer.

When you sell to local customers, be prepared for slow payments. Getting paid on time — and sometimes at all — can be a huge problem. We have seen several companies, including subsidiaries of Fortune-500 corporations, flounder in China because they let accounts receivables slip for too long.

You need to start internally. The legacy of the planned economy means that there is little understanding for the cost of capital — "a sale is a sale, we have a contract and sooner or later we will get paid". Making sure that your own organization, especially the sales department, understands the importance of prompt payments from customers will be your first challenge.

Anders remembers a discussion with a senior sales person in the early days of the company. The sales representative had made three large deliveries of cutting tools to a customer which was now four months in arrears on the first invoice. After a long discussion on the importance of collecting this money, the sales rep noted that "I understand that we need to get paid, but the customer just doesn't have the money right now". "But we checked that he pays salaries to his employees?", Anders said. "Yes", the sales rep replied, "we did check that before we sold to him". "And last time you were there, was the electricity on in the office?" "It was". "So maybe he does have some money after all, he's just not using it to pay us?" He reluctantly agreed that this was indeed probably the case and went back to successfully collect the three payments before our next delivery was made.

Customers and clients will let payment schedules slip for a number of reasons: Because they, too, lack an understanding for the importance of collecting on accounts receivables; because they tend to be owed money by their own customers; because they are deliberately trying to improve their cash balance or because they will simply wait for you to raise a fuss before paying. Customers will refuse to pay interest on late payments, and even threaten to take away their business if you push them too hard on getting paid according to the terms in the contract. This was a problem at Eastwei even when serving mainly multinational companies in China — slow payments and a lack of respect for the contractual obligations of the "stronger" party pervades organizations.

If you want to foster a healthy credit culture among your customers, you need to be firm to the point of punctiliousness in demanding on-time payments for goods delivered. You need to engender respect by showing that you care about getting paid on time and are prepared to risk further sales in order to get your money from earlier orders. Private Chinese companies understand that they actively need to manage their credit risk. When Eastwei was late paying a large sum of money to a first-time vendor because our client, in turn, was not paying in time, we received a visit from the vendor's whole management team who simply sat down in our meeting room and refused to leave until we had outlined clear measures for collecting, and forwarding, the outstanding money. The polite determination of the vendor was impressive and several years later we are still doing business with them.

In Sandvik, we devoted a great deal of effort to getting this right at the outset. Setting a standard and showing that you are prepared to stick to it is much easier to do at the early stages of a business relationship. Letting debts deteriorate and then trying to push the customer when things have already gotten out of hand does not build respect and is much more difficult. Remember that customers usually do pay some of their debtors — the trick is to make sure your company is one of the parties getting paid.

It is difficult for a sales person in any country to ask the customer for payment, but our feeling is that this is particularly so in China. Coaching sales representatives on how to make this less dramatic can help a lot. When speaking to Sandvik sales people about this issue, we often put the issue in the context of mutual respect and face-giving: "We have a contract with the customer where we have promised to deliver certain products of good quality according to a certain schedule. In the same contract, the customer has promised to pay for those products, also according to a time schedule. We have now delivered our part, on time, and the customer is happy with the products. It is therefore natural that the customer should also keep his part of the agreement by paying on time". The formulation may look naive, but framing the issue like this proved very helpful for our sales people because it made them feel justified in asking for the money.

10.8. Checklist for Collecting Payments

Every company in China must take the following steps to ensure that accounts receivables from sales do not become a debilitating burden:

- *Be firm from the outset*: If you have a problem, be strict from the beginning. It is difficult to change the behavior of an established relationship. Ernst Behrens of Siemens notes that "Chinese customers respect strength. Japanese and American companies have been more stringent about payments and more prone to take customers to court over accounts receivable, even in the face of threats losing future business. Europeans companies have been punished because Chinese companies have taken advantage of them".
- *Ask for payments in advance*: You should try to get paid upfront, or at least receive some sort of guarantee such as a letter of credit. In the event that this is not possible, but you still want to do business with the customer, start by fulfilling smaller orders and let these grow as the customer builds a record of paying on time.
- *Communicate the urgency internally*: Make your own colleagues understand the costs of not getting paid on time — explain the costs of capital and why it is better to have the money productively invested in the operations, rather having them locked up in noncontributing accounts receivables. Sometimes, you may need to resort to concrete pictures: "the unpaid sum equals the

cost of two machines in our factory, which could now be producing products...".

- *Coach the sales people*: To try to make asking for money less dramatic for them by emphasizing the mutuality of your agreements with customers.
- *Showcase examples from your own vendors*: At Sandvik, we found that we, as an unknown company to a new supplier, were often asked to pay in advance. Almost all new suppliers asked to be paid at least partly in advance, usually with the rest of the payment due on delivery. By communicating the policies of our vendors to our own sales people, we created an understanding for the business realities involved and provided them with arguments for using with their own customers.
- *Establish your own credit rankings*: Without access to external rankings, your best bet is to create a clear system yourself by observing the payment patterns of each customer.
- *Tie sales commissions to payment*: If a commission is paid to sales persons as part of an incentive package, this commission should not be paid related to invoiced sales, but to paid sales.

Chapter 11

Marketing to China

For years now, China has been developing into an inexpensive production base for export manufacturing. But as the Chinese economy grows, more and more companies arrive mainly to sell to Chinese customers; they want to market their products in China.

A simple definition of marketing looks like this: finding customers, creating products that they will buy, and effectively communicating with them so that one can sell as much as possible to them (here and throughout, we have chosen to talk about "products" rather than belaboring the reader with terms like "products and services" — we are sure it will be obvious when we mean both).

By "marketing", then, we simply mean how we can grab as large a (profitable) share of the Chinese wallet as possible for our companies. But how does one go about making a killing in China? As we have seen, many people have emphasized the importance of political relationships, so-called "guanxi", and other nontraditional aspects of marketing. Relationships are (and will probably remain) important in China, but in most industries they are no longer the key to success. China of the 21st century is different from the Chinese marketplace of the 1980s.

Today, China is rapidly turning into a market economy. It is arguably also one of the most competitive markets in the world: you will often be challenged locally by *all* your global competitors (American, European, Japanese, and Korean), as well as increasingly savvy Chinese companies. In the business confidence surveys carried out by European Chambers of Commerce in China, "tough competitive environment" has regularly come up as the leading obstacle to profitability, ahead of other barriers more often mentioned by the media, such as "bureaucracy" or "corruption".

Chinese customers are picky, because they can choose between products from the best suppliers in the world. Most international firms now realize that you cannot market old technology to China — local customers are looking for cutting-edge stuff, especially in the industrial arena. Local service levels also tend to be high — some of the companies we have worked with have used China as the benchmark for their worldwide service offering, since the local market is perceived to be the most demanding in the world for after-sales service. For years, excellent service was a way for Chinese manufacturers to compensate for product quality problems; now, as quality has gone up, service still continues to give a competitive edge.

The market is regionally fragmented (consumers in Guangzhou tend to like different products and designs than consumers in Beijing, and those in Shanghai have yet another set of preferences); rather than view China as one market, you should see it as somewhat akin to Europe. It is also fast-moving (Chinese managers often complain about the plodding pace at corporate headquarters in the USA and Europe) because it is in a constant state of flux as China accelerates to catch up with trends in the rest of the world (what sold yesterday is no longer attractive today and will be hopelessly outmoded tomorrow). This is especially true for consumer goods, but even B2B suppliers frequently see different demand and customer profiles in different parts of the country.

Against such a background, it is actually possible to argue that there is no fundamental difference between marketing in China and marketing in other countries — you may just have to be an even better marketer, and have even more focus and endurance, in order to succeed. You need to have your ear to the ground and watch your step, even as you are running to keep up with the fast-paced market.

Of course, one can claim that guanxi and government relations are of paramount importance in certain industries, for example telecoms and other infrastructure. But this is not unique to China: Ericsson's work with British Telecom features as a case study in modern relationship marketing textbooks. Many of those who tout the importance of guanxi networks are consultants with roots in the last century, when China was still a planned economy, or expatriate Chinese whose only unique sales point in applying for a job with your organization may be their claim to "know the Mayor of Longweiawei" (although this particular city is of our own invention, we have lost count of all the real-world people who have tried to sell their services to us or our clients mainly on account of similar relationships).

In our opinion, success in China relies on the same tried and true methods that we use in more familiar markets. But there is no room for complacency — even as we offer the best products in our portfolio to satisfy the tastes of the choosy Chinese customer, we must also utilize the most sophisticated approaches in our global marketing arsenal if we are to be worthy of his or her attention.

11.1. The Ear to the Ground — Understanding Chinese Customers

Just like the Indian in a classic Western, the heroes of the Chinese adventure movie *Warriors between Heaven and Earth* listen with their ears to the ground in order to determine just how many of the emperor's pursuing riders are on the approach. Knowing the lay of the land is as important on the marketing battlefield, where enemy products compete with yours for the money of consumers, as when you are waging a real war and the imperial troops are about to overrun your little band of brigands.

Together with his colleagues at Eastwei Relations, Johan has marketed a wide variety of stuff in China, from Swiss watches and hospital sterilizers to radiator materials and vodka. Every time they are assigned a new marketing mission, the consultants ask the client to describe his or her typical Chinese customer. Surprisingly often, they get an answer along the lines of "female, 20–45 years of age, above average income and education".

In order to communicate and sell a product (not to mention create it in the first place), we need to have an in-depth understanding of our customers. Demographics like age, sex, and income (for business-to-business customers: size, industry, and profitability) are not enough. Which are the values, needs, and trends that make your customers tick? How do they live, what do they believe in…, and what does the 20–45-year-old woman with above-average income dream about?

It is especially difficult to understand the mindset of customers when one's own background is totally different from theirs. The culture, values, and experiences of Chinese customers and consumers will be far removed from those of the expatriate manager. Their needs, preferences, and concerns will consequently be different too.

Hiring a Chinese marketing manager is no patent solution. She may know her compatriots (or rather, as we shall see, her compatriots from the same city) better than you, but on the other hand she may lack the world-class experience of your own business that an experienced expatriate coworker can bring. Chinese customers are, as are those in other countries, unique individuals; besides, they live in a dynamic and rapidly changing marketplace. In order to understand them, we need the same refined research methods that we use on more mature markets.

11.1.1. *The fridge in the bedroom*

One of Eastwei's longest-standing clients in China is Electrolux, the world's largest white goods company. When Electrolux first started selling refrigerators in China, the Eastwei team, together with a research company, carried out a so-called *Problem Detection Study* in China. The aim of this simple yet ingenious methodology is to identify the main problems that consumers encounter in buying or

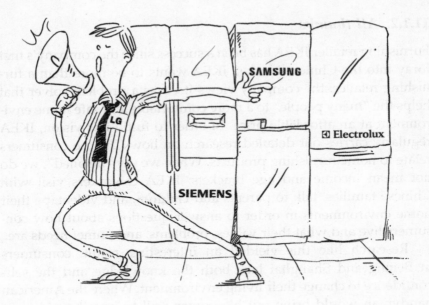

using a product, the idea of course being to find smart ways of addressing these issues and thus beat the competition.

When consumers were asked to rank a couple of hundred different problems (ranging from "I worry about my fridge being scratched during the transport to my home" to "Refrigerators consume too much electricity"), several of the ten top-ranking problems were related to noise and vibrations. The explanation turned out to be simple: Chinese kitchens are often too small to fit the family refrigerator, so consumers tend to place the fridge next to the TV couch, or even in their bedroom. Cramped Chinese consumers may be more used to living with noise than privacy-spoiled Westerners, but they are no happier than we are about waking up in the middle of the night when the compressor clatters to life.

This consumer insight led Electrolux to develop an especially silent refrigerator, which was sold using the slogan "listen before you buy". The product became a sales breakthrough for Electrolux on the Chinese market.

11.1.2. *All thumbs*

Furnishing retailer IKEA has been a success since the company's first foray into the Chinese market. IKEA wants to be more than a furnishing retailer; the company views itself as a problem solver that helps the "many people" to a more comfortable and safe home environment at an affordable price. In order to fulfill this vision, IKEA regularly carries out detailed research on how Chinese consumers relate to home furnishing products. When we say "detailed", we do not mean income and age brackets: IKEA coworkers visit with Chinese families, talk to parents and children, and videotape their home environments in order to answer questions about how consumers live and what their values, problems, and unmet needs are.

Research like this yielded an interesting result: consumers in Beijing and Shanghai lack both the knowledge and the self-confidence to change their living environment. Where the American handyman would bring out his power drill to install a nice coat hanger, the typical Chinese consumer bundled the family jackets on a chair in the hallway: "I don't have a drill, I'm afraid I'll destroy the walls, and anyway I plan to wait until I buy a new apartment — this old one is impossible to do much with in the first place" was a typical consumer comment.

In order to build interest in home furnishing and home improvement, Eastwei produced 52 episodes of a weekly TV show for broadcast in Beijing and Shanghai. In the program, we visited Chinese families and asked them how they would like to change their homes. Using a relaxed, humorous tone of voice, we then proceeded to do "before/after"-style makeovers where we showed simple solutions to storage problems, improved lighting, or simply made a room more cozy or practical. The TV show was a huge success for IKEA, because it fulfilled a very real need for the Chinese consumer.

11.1.3. *Are there cultural differences in*
marketing communications?

Do you need to consider cultural differences when doing marketing communications in China? Our personal belief is that the words "cultural differences" tend to make us focus on the wrong things; as we argue above, it is all about understanding individual consumers rather than abstract "cultural" traits.

In practice, regional differences within China tend to be as important as differences from consumers in other countries. In working with the Swiss watch brand Omega, the Eastwei team quickly had to learn which watches sell where: sporty, cool models in the south, diamond studded miniature timepieces in central China, and massive gold affairs in the north. Naturally, we had to adjust marketing activities to suit these products as well as other local preferences.

There are, however, political sensitivities. When a major international agency produced an ad for the Toyota Landcruiser, they were flamed in Chinese chat groups and viciously attacked by journalists: the ads showed traditional Chinese lions bowing to the cars with taglines such as "a car that demands respect". Consumers deemed the advertising insulting; China and Japan have had a complicated relationship ever since WWII, where Japan has refused to apologize for war crimes during the invasion of China.

A basic "cultural difference" we need to take into account is, of course, language. Industrial companies sometimes ask us if they can simply use marketing materials in English — after all, their customers are well-educated engineers with good foreign language skills. Our advice is always the same: even though some Chinese customer groups read English fluently, they always prefer their mother tongue. By providing information in Chinese, you ensure that customers understand, pick up, and remember your message.

11.1.4. *Checklist — Understanding customers*

In summary, here is some good advice to anyone who would like to understand their Chinese customers:

- *Customers are not just "Chinese"*: They are Cantonese, Shanghaiese, Beijingers, and so on. Regional differences within China are often as large as those between European countries (and the Chinese "dialects", our linguist friends tell us, are often more distinct than, say, English and French).

- *Do extensive market research — but not just of the "percentage" kind*: What you really need to know, you cannot glean from a table of numbers. Use an agency that can help you set up focus groups and in-depth interviews — and make sure you are there behind the one-way glass so that you get first-hand impressions of your target group under conditions where they are not being polite, telling you what you want to hear. Or do what Procter & Gamble did: ask last-year students of the Chinese film academy to make a documentary on teenage values and lifestyles. The results turned out to be a nice complement to traditional market research, and were highly relevant to the sales strategy.
- *Talk to customers*: Market research can complement your own gut feeling, but never replace it. Johan often, for example, sets up CEO visits to Chinese homes for fortune-500 companies — a simple, inexpensive way of getting a feel for the market. When his colleagues at Eastwei draft a market plan, they always talk directly to the customers of clients, in order to get an emotional feel for what the traditional market research is really saying.
- *Make sure you have translators that can really convey the nuances of research and communications messaging*: You would be surprised at how often we see "literal" translations that miss the point — both of what your customers are trying to tell you, and what you are trying to tell them.

No matter how much money you spend, you will not advertise your way into the heart of the Chinese consumer. Real marketing is, as we all know, about understanding the needs of consumers, and meeting those needs more effectively than our competitors.

The first consideration in doing this is the product portfolio.

11.2. Product Portfolio

For years, foreign companies tended to fit their Chinese factories with older production equipment capable of producing mid- or low-range products. The resulting market strategy was often problematic from the outset: the locally produced products would compete with state-of-the-art imported alternatives on the one hand, and inexpensive products manufactured by Chinese companies on the other. Customers wanting what they perceived to be "the best" would buy the imported goods, while cost-conscious customers would buy local manufactures. This product position led to what we have come to call "the valley of death" — a no-man's land where volume is under pressure from cheaper goods while profits are reaped by more upscale competitors. We see examples of such polarization in almost every industry in China.

A premium position may pose greater needs for educating customers. In industrial marketing, you may need to introduce concepts that are novel to local industries: lifecycle thinking, increased productivity, and so on. At Sandvik, Anders worked hard to train sales people in selling the productivity angle. This often entailed finding very concrete benefits and explaining them through concrete examples: "If you have five machines and buy our Sandvik tools which raise the productivity of these machines by 20%, you don't have to buy the sixth machine!" Since capital for new investments has periodically been hard to find in Chinese industries with low margins, such an argument could prove quite persuasive.

To sum up, there are several reasons why a premium product portfolio usually makes sense for foreign companies in China:

- Chinese customers, both in consumer goods and industrial marketing, are usually brand- and quality-conscious, and they have a lot of choice. Face and prestige do enter the equation.
- In case strategy needs to change, it is always easier to move from a premium position into the mid range than vice versa.
- Premium products often embody the core benefits of your offering.
- Even though it may require educating customers, a narrow product portfolio is easier to explain and also makes it easier to get your own sales organization up to speed.

11.3. "Very Cheap, Very Cheap" — Pricing Strategies

For a high-end product strategy to work, prices need to be high. Is it really possible to succeed with a premium price strategy in China?

If we are to believe Chinese salesmen, sales in China is almost always about price (and the impression becomes even more compelling as you sit through negotiations with a Chinese corporate customer).

In China, bargaining is a national sport; in no other country we have experienced people trying to round the restaurant bill off *downwards* after dinner. Because of the cut-throat market environment, Chinese companies also tend to compete on price. But this is a dangerous path to take, and foreign companies have paid dearly for their attempts to undersell local competitors with a lower cost base.

The pricing issue is not just an issue for foreign companies in China — it has plagued local competitors, even whole industries, in the country. Price wars have been due to bad management, flawed investment decisions stemming from a lack of understanding of the cost of capital, industry overcapacity legacies, and regional protectionism — just try to sell a taxi in Shanghai if you are not Volkswagen offering a Santana. In such a pressured environment, a quality or market leader can almost be said to have a moral responsibility to also be a price leader, in order to ensure the health of the whole industry.

You will need to persuade your sales team, perhaps by pointing out that the Chinese consume more Remy Martin and Martell than any other country (if they reply "maybe they just like it", consider the fact that it is consumed in tumblers to wash down a spicy dinner), or that the number of Rolex and Omega watches is totally out of proportion to the country's GDP, or maybe that customers in the 1990s continued to buy imported luxury cars in spite of a 170% import tariff, even as excellent local joint-venture cars were widely available. Some consumer goods companies, such as Häagen-Dasz, have chosen a significantly more premium pricing strategy in

China than on their home markets — sometimes in spite of the fact that the products are manufactured in China at a lower cost!

It should be obvious that Chinese consumer psychology is the same as everywhere else in the world. If a customer perceives that he is getting a better deal (which may be intangible — Chinese *love* brand-name goods!), he or she will be willing to pay something extra. As you enter the market, you have a one-time chance to establish a price structure that ensures long-term profitability in China.

11.4. Why Brand is So Important

Johan remembers when, as a student, he bought his first Chinese bicycle. Johan had his eye on a Flying Pigeon — a shiny green bike which, at the time, was the Mercedes of bikes in China. After saving a month's worth of scholarship money, Johan traveled by bus for an hour from the Peking University campus outside Beijing to visit a large store on Wangfujing in the Beijing city center to buy his bike and started treading his way home. Halfway to the campus, Johan heard a strange clattering noise and turned around to discover that he had been leaving a trail of nuts, bolts, and other spare parts along the way from the store.

In general, brand is important in China. One reason is the "trust deficit" illustrated by Johan's bike purchase. We have already mentioned this several times, for example in the context of negotiations and recruitment. But there are also other reasons:

- Asians are preoccupied with face and prestige; this applies even to B2B products.
- The market is usually fragmented, making a strong brand a competitive opportunity.
- As we have seen, employees care a lot about working for a "reputable company".

In the following section, we will look at how to build a brand efficiently in China.

11.5. PR and Advertising

For several decades, the communications professional in China had two simple tools at his disposal: force your audience to listen, and prohibit all alternative messages. Using the state-controlled media, with the stated objective of indoctrinating the populace in "right thinking", and propaganda meetings where citizens were forced to sit through endless political rhetoric, the authorities succeeded in familiarizing most people with the politically correct agenda of the moment. A strong authoritarian tradition, and a school system where professors pontificate to diligently note-taking students, have reinforced these tendencies to one-way communication.

But just as a planned economy results in inefficient allocation of resources and to awkward products, a monopoly on opinion seems to lead to bad communications.

During the 1980s and 1990s, the quality of Chinese advertising (including that produced by international agencies in China) was generally low. Lacking the professional acumen to position the unique benefits of individual products, and the creativity to communicate them in an interesting way, companies tended to use beautiful women: if you open a Chinese in-flight magazine, you will still find numerous me-too consumer electronics products flanked by smiling beauties, accompanied by an explanatory text stating that the lady in the picture is "world-famous movie star/singer/model this-or-that", just in case readers do not recognize the "celebrity". Other popular advertising components have been kitschy mountainscapes, well-known European tourist destinations, and Mona Lisas. In the same vein, industrial companies have tended to produce marketing material which look more like technical spec sheets than compelling presentations of the unique sales points and benefits of their products.

The low quality of market communications actually gives marketers in China a unique chance to differentiate their offering. On this competitive market, where hundreds of me-too products fight for consumer attention, the communicative noise level is not yet on a par with more mature media markets. But in order to differentiate successfully, marketers must not only, as we have discussed above, understand the values and needs of their Chinese consumers, but also demand the same creativity from their agencies as they do back home.

There is plenty of room for creativity not only in advertising content, but also in finding innovative communications channels. The IKEA TV show is one example. Car companies have found a good channel in elevator billboards at exclusive developments. And cool brands like ABSOLUT Vodka are beginning to exploit interactive media to reach their narrowly targeted consumer segments. When looking at the huge mass of mainstream consumers, do not forget how sophisticated certain niche groups and trend setters can be.

Some key points to pay attention to as you start communicating with Chinese customers:

- choose the right channels;
- find a locally savvy agency that can provide really creative ideas;
- build a long-term relationship with your agency partner so that they understand what your company and products stand for.

11.6. Public Relations

In China, all media are state owned — but they are all financed by advertising revenues. In other words, there is no real public service channel in China... or maybe they all are?

This is a typical example of the paradoxes that foreign businesses meet on the Chinese market. What are the behind-the-scenes dynamics at Chinese media, and how should one go about working with journalists to create successful PR campaigns in China?

11.6.1. *A changing media scene*

Since the mid-1980s, the Chinese media industry has grown rapidly. Television is the most important consumer medium, with a thousand or so channels fighting for audience attention; the top ones, for example China Central Television (CCTV), are billion-dollar businesses with enormous influence over consumers. Local stations have smaller reach, but tend to have higher ratings than CCTV in their home cities and provinces: Beijing TV (BTV) and Shanghai TV (STV) each boasts about 10 channels. And in Guangzhou, people tend to watch the Hong Kong channels more than either CCTV or the local Guangdong offerings.

Newspapers are also important. People's Daily has the highest circulation, several million copies. (This does not mean that this Party mouthpiece is actually the most read publication, though — the high circulation derives from the fact that government workplaces traditionally subscribe to a fixed number of copies). Circulation estimates of more commercial papers in China can sometimes be undependable, since advertising departments tend to inflate figures to make more money. But there is a large number of local and national newspapers that are really popular with readers, and more are launched each month. Some of these are pure news media, whereas others cover a certain industry.

Magazines have quickly multiplied. A number of international media groups are already present through joint ventures or licensing agreements with Chinese publishers; today you can read Elle and Cosmopolitan as well as Fortune and Forbes in Chinese editions. Local magazines have also mushroomed, and some have earned international fame: Caijing, a feisty magazine that scrutinizes companies listed on Chinese exchanges, has made its name by exposing shady insider deals and other activities that are detrimental to shareholder interests. The preponderance of local publications is readily apparent from any of the many magazine stalls dotting every Chinese city.

For advertising agencies, media planning (where to place your ads for maximum impact with a certain target group) is a great challenge. Since circulation figures can be doctored, and in any case tend to change quickly, media planning is sometimes more of an art than a science in China. You need to work with proactive and creative people who understand the intricacies of the local media.

And you need to give them enough freedom to quickly grab bargain placement opportunities when they appear.

Industry media are especially interesting, especially for the Business-to-business market. Since most Chinese customer groups have a hard time reading English, Chinese decision makers tend to get their information through local industry publications. In some heavily globalized areas, IT for example, one will find Chinese editions of well-known magazines such as PC World. In other industries, media are often published by local associations or research institutes.

One of our clients, Outokumpu, has skillfully utilized such media to build decision maker understanding of copper radiator technology and how environmental trends and regulations will impact the future of the heat exchanger industry. After several years of such education efforts, Outokumpu has increasingly become perceived as a thought leader and source of information for industry journalists, generating further coverage as media ask the company to comment on technical developments and other trends.

11.6.2. *Internet*

The fast growth of internet use in China means it now warrants its own topic in any discussion of Chinese marketing. Numbers tend to become outdated quickly; suffice it to say that there are more Chinese mobile phone users than any other nationality. Analysts believe there will be more Chinese than English web pages in a few years' time.

The internet has already recast entire business areas in China. The computer gaming business, for example, hobbled along for years as PC-ROM's were pirated without revenues for game developers. The advent of networked games created a new revenue model as users paid for subscriptions, and the industry has grown in only a couple of years from close to zero to hundreds of millions of dollars. Creative marketers also use the internet to communicate and establish dialogue with end users, just as in more developed markets.

11.6.3. *The influence of politics*

During his own training as TV presenter at Beijing TV, Johan learned that the role of the journalist is to be the "throat and tongue" of the authorities. When Johan produced music video shows in the mid-1990s, his boss at the station vetted each program to make sure it was politically correct before broadcast.

With the increasing liberalization of society, things are changing. Chinese media are becoming more and more similar to their Western counterparts: hungry for sensation, and increasingly critical of societal problems like corruption and abuse of power. But the state still puts limits on what a Chinese journalist can and cannot write, especially concerning the country's leadership.

The government has at its disposition an effective apparatus for control to make sure that media stay within the established boundaries. The Publicity Department has at its disposal hordes of retired party functionaries to watch TV and read newspapers, and to report inappropriate content. The system works: during his time as TV host, Johan was reprimanded on several occasions for choosing wordings or other content that was deemed unsuitable for television. A large company had to recall a million catalogues when it turned out that they had forgotten to include a small island off the country's southern coast on their map of China (Taiwan was included, but little Hainan was missing) — a kind of omission that is always politically sensitive because it is seen as a challenge to the integrity of motherland. The company hired a bunch of students that dotted the island onto the maps so that the catalog could be distributed in the end.

Lacking juicy political scandals to report on, and not daring to challenge well-connected local companies, Chinese journalists often target international companies for negative reporting. The headline "big bad foreign company mistreats little Chinese consumer" tends to get the same front page treatment in China as "the clergyman's secret orgies" would in the West. For historical reasons, Japanese companies have been especially prone to such attacks, but companies like Daimler-Chrysler have also ended up in hot water: a dissatisfied car customer recently gave the gathered local press a field day by using a donkey to drag his Mercedes around town, after having first demolished the poor car with a sledge hammer.

Another consequence of the monopoly on official information is the rampant spread of rumors and urban myths in China. During the SARS epidemic, these rumors reached epic proportions ("tonight we will stay inside — the air force will bomb Beijing with disinfectant") but the phenomenon is important enough to have a special name: "xiaodao xiaoxi" or "street news". Not only politics and epidemics are discussed through these informal channels: consumers and industrial customers tend to rely heavily on word of mouth about products and companies. This trend will continue as the mobile internet is rolled out in China. You need to be tuned into these informal channels, such as internet chat rooms, if you are to quickly pick up on market signals.

11.6.4. *Media relations are a great marketing tool in China*

Strategic PR is an effective way for companies targeting consumers or corporate customers to market products while building long-term brand equity in China — and it is also a proactive defense against media issues escalating into crises. So what is needed to implement an effective program?

We have already talked about having the right message for the target group in question — but you also need personal relations with journalists, to communicate your company and its products from a wider industry perspective, to try to find a Chinese angle, and to use language and pictures that are easy for your target group to identify with. Taken together, these requirements mean you need to build your PR strategy for the long term.

11.6.5. *Building knowledge-driven media relations*

Chinese journalists, like Chinese professionals in general, want a personal relationship with the companies and organizations that they cover. The foundation of strong relationships is regular contacts, keeping the other party informed, and making them feel important and appreciated.

Regular contacts do not just support the relationship. In a society developing at the breakneck speed of China, journalists are not always up-to-date on the worldwide developments in your particular line of business. You need to keep them continuously informed of new trends, new products, and of your company's vision for the future of the industry. In this way, you take the high ground and become seen as a thought leader and credible source of information in your sphere.

Journalists are your conduit to readers — but getting published is no guarantee that your message is clear, relevant, or interesting to your target group. The information you disseminate should be given a Chinese angle, tied to the local perspective. You need to express yourself in comprehensible terms and find formulations that stir your audience to action.

11.7. Guanxi and Marketing in China

We have, in several places, touched on the importance of relationships, *guanxi*, for everyone who wants to successfully do business in China. The concept of *guanxi* is especially important in industrial, or B2B, marketing — to do business, you need to spend time on building good relationships with individuals in your customers' organizations. In sales, guanxi is almost synonymous with building trust.

As we have pointed out before, there is nothing mysterious or idiosyncratic to China about this. During the 1990s, Relationship Marketing, RM, became a buzzword around the world. Applying RM best practices in China will go a long way to make your industrial marketing effort effective.

11.7.1. *A call center to sell call centers*

A few years ago, Johan took a phone call from a major telecom provider, who had sold thousands of switchboards on the Chinese market. The company felt that it was losing touch with its installed base, and asked Johan and his colleagues for a quotation to set up a customer newsletter.

After talking to a number of the client's customers, it became clear that there was no lack of printed information — but the customers did complain about a lack of regular contacts, and felt it was difficult to get help with upgrades and new technical solutions.

The problem turned out to be rooted in a classical phenomenon: sales people are notoriously reluctant to share customer information (especially with other sales people, and even more so in China). This often leads to incomplete and outdated customer registers, and even to the company losing contact with customers when salesmen leave the company, taking their rolodexes with them. We found the same to be true in this case.

Instead of a newsletter, Johan suggested another solution. The client had a service department staffed by four (pretty worn-out) engineers who received dozens of service calls daily. We added one more engineer to the service team, freeing each of the engineers up for a day a week to do proactive outreach to customers. During each call, they asked if the equipment was functioning smoothly and at the same time confirmed or corrected contact information and equipment specifications in the customer database.

Within a few months, the service group turned into a sales machine. In the service call context, customers became receptive to discussing upgrades and paid service programs. As the service group proactively called more and more customers, the number of incoming service calls declined, freeing up even more time for proactive calling and so on in a virtuous cycle. According to the service engineers, customers were especially happy with the personal contact established — a classical example of how to use CRM methods to grow sales by building stronger bonds with customers.

11.8. Branding with Chinese Characters

Chinese characters carry both meaning and sound. Most brand names, such as Motorola ("Motuoluola") have been translated phonetically, and others have been translated for meaning (Microsoft is known as "Wei Ruan", "wei" meaning "micro" and "ruan" meaning "soft"). There is no one way of translating your brand name — the best way has to be chosen from case to case, depending on how the name will be used and what it should communicate in the Chinese-speaking world.

Companies who do not actively choose and promote a Chinese brand name will get one anyway. Since it is so difficult for most Chinese speakers to use and remember English names, Chinese media will automatically write a "translation" of the brand with Chinese characters. Chinese names are therefore very important in China and parts of Asia. This has several consequences:

- Once the Chinese name has established itself, it may be hard to root out if it should not be the one you prefer, or one that cannot be registered.
- Because of trademark laws the company may lose the right to the most "popular" Chinese version of a corporate or product name. There are many examples. A recent and famous one being Viagra, which because of large media coverage quickly became famous in China — the translation favored by the media was "Weige", which means "Big Brother", "brother" being slang for the male reproductive organ. A local competitor registered this familiar Chinese translation before Pfizer had the chance to react.

It is hard to win a court case for a Chinese name like this, since there are many conceivable translations of the original English name.

Today it is also possible to register Chinese-character domain names. If you do not want to invite the name-nappers and lose the right to your own internet brand in China and Asia, you had better start thinking of what to register.

11.9. Brand Names Make a Difference

In the West, brand names are used as positioning statements. A good name saves advertising dollars, which is why consumer companies will put so much money and effort into choosing their product brand names — a name like "Head and Shoulders" clearly supports the brand's positioning.

Multinational companies often make mistakes when they try to adapt their corporate and product names for the Chinese market. These mistakes are costly. Fortune-500 companies have spent millions trying to correct naming errors.

There will often be internal conflicts because of dubious names. This is because the name is so central to the marketing and positioning, and because it is difficult to prove right and wrong, especially when the local top management is made up of expatriates who do not speak Chinese. Names concern most coworkers; everyone tends to have an opinion, leading to drawn-out discussions within the company.

11.10. Chinese is Unique

Since Chinese is pronounced so differently from Western languages, it is often difficult to find a name that sounds familiar. There are a number of Chinese dialects, and a name that sounds similar in Mandarin may not sound at all the same when the characters are pronounced in Cantonese. In this case, it may be better to go for a "Microsoft" solution, where the English and Chinese names are kept clearly phonetically different, and the name instead retains the *meaning* of the original.

If it is not similar enough, a phonetically similar name may actually *weaken* your international brand name by reinforcing an "almost right" pronunciation.

11.11. Mainland China, Taiwan, and HK

In a networked world, cultural affinities are becoming more important than political borders. Important Chinese-speaking regions include Taiwan, Singapore, Hong Kong, and the economically influential Chinese minorities in Asia, Australia, and the USA. People in all these regions are increasingly sharing the same media and sources of information, but the actual Chinese characters are somewhat different. A Chinese brand name that takes these differences into account can save a great deal of money in future packaging and advertising costs.

11.12. A Few Steps to Successful Marketing in China

- *Be humble*: Make sure you do your market research twice as diligently as you would at home, and get out of your office to meet personally with Chinese consumers so that you get in touch with their everyday reality.
- *Do not be afraid to show who you are — but do adapt your communication*: Foreign business can be so keen to adapt themselves that they sacrifice core values. Remember that you are in China not to be another local company, but to offer something new and unique to the local marketplace. Still, you need to adopt the right tone of voice and chose the right language for Chinese people to perceive you in the way you would like to be seen. This means describing your own company and product offering in a context which is intelligible to Chinese customers, whose needs and frame of reference may be different from your own.
- *Trust your own judgment*: Even if China is different, common sense combined with in-depth analysis of the market will get you a long way.
- *Get yourself a Chinese company name… and one for yourself as well*: No Chinese person can pronounce, remember or relate to a name like "Björkstén" (which is why Johan's Chinese name is Dalong, "Big Dragon").
- *Build networks*: Be diligent and structured about mapping and maintaining all business and government relations that may be valuable to your business activities. Do not throw away name cards — save them along with careful notes of where you met the person, and what you talked about.
- *Demand the same quality in market communications as you would at home*: Choose great local PR and advertising agencies and

challenge them with the same demands for strategically sound, sophisticated creativity that you would in the US or Europe.

- *Build relationships with Chinese journalists*: They are a wonderful communications channel for reaching Chinese customers, but also an important source of market information. This is particularly true for Business-to-business companies.
- *Be realistic*: Your products may not suit needs over all of China, and you may not have the logistics to distribute them all over this giant market. Better focus on one or two local markets and build from there.
- *Take an interest in China*: If you want to be a locally savvy marketer, you need to truly care about your customers and the country you are working in. As part of the deal, you will be privy to a ceaseless source of fascination — the meeting with a culture spanning millennia.

Chapter 12

Successful Execution Demands Top Management Attention

We have looked at some of the cultural and societal factors that influence management in China, and how these place specific demands on the recruiting and development of Chinese coworkers. But this environmental backdrop also influences the day-to-day practice of leadership and management. Most expatriate managers feel that, in order to be successful in China, they need to be more hands-on, personally involve themselves in more detailed issues, and put in place stronger and more structured follow-up systems in China than what they are used to from other markets.

The reasons for this are:

- The psychology of Chinese coworkers.
- The opportunities for misunderstandings — linguistic and cultural.
- The lack of trust.

12.1. Execution Requires High-Level, Hands-on Senior Management Attention, and Follow-Up

In previous chapters, we have come face to face with some of the everyday challenges of managing a Chinese company. The point of departure for most Chinese employees tends to be asking the boss for advice, or, barring that, carefully consider what the boss

would most probably like them to say or do. For the manager of a multinational company, this can create problems and clashes with the rest of the global organization. In short, many Western managers will feel that Chinese coworkers will deal with certain situations differently than colleagues on other markets.

- Superficially "agree" with the boss, but then fail to implement a decision.
- Interpret the letter, rather than the spirit, of decisions and regulations.
- Dislike making mistakes, go to great lengths to avoid doing so and try to avoid confronting management with problems for as long as possible.

On the surface, such behavior may simply seem irresponsible. But if you look at the educational and social background of your coworkers, it becomes easier to understand. The so-called "situational leadership" model emphasizes that different employees require different management styles not only depending on individual characteristics, but also their maturity in a particular job role. If you are familiar with this model, it can provide a useful framework for considering management challenges in China. An immature coworker requires encouragement and help in building self-confidence, as well as more hands-on, directive management. Giving the right — not too much, and not too little — support at the different stages of a junior colleague's development will speed up his or her growth and motivation for doing a good job.

Preventing malfeasance is another strong imperative for being more hands-on. Peter Humphrey comments that "if you are always around, clearly visible, even just going down to the shop floor to say hello, you will be seen to care about the organization". Conversely, a hands-off attitude can be interpreted as "he's not watching" and invite problems. "Very often head office or a senior expatriate manager... do not show that they actually care about their operation, they are unable to reach out to all levels of employees, and they over-rely on a single point of reporting".

12.2. You Need to Create a Trusting and Accepting Culture

Most companies require employees to show initiative, to be proactive, to take initiative and to accept responsibility for problems and mistakes. Fostering such attitudes in your Chinese workforce requires a long-term educational and trust-building process: We must create an environment where people dare to make decisions. Employees must feel free and secure enough to make mistakes.

Sony's Country Manager in China, Mr. Kawasaki, offers the following advice: "Corporate culture is very important, especially accepting challenges — and failure. Chinese people are more afraid of making mistakes than people in other countries. They will try to explain away errors or justify themselves. It is important to create a culture which encourages people to accept challenges and does not punish mistakes".

Remember that you are fighting against authoritarian tradition as well as an educational system which emphasizes rote learning rather than critical evaluation and thinking. China has an excellent educational system, but it fails to develop the analytical and critical skills that multinational companies require.

12.3. Attaining Hands-Off

Management in a newly started company in China is by nature always more hands-on, involved and engaged, than in a long established company in the West. It is however important that we control this "engagement", so that we create space for our local people to grow. If we, as managers, take all decisions and responsibility, there will be little left for our local employees to do. Just as in the West, employees will be frustrated and we as managers will be stressed by all we have to do. Hands-on management should be more "involved" than "directive".

It is also good to build up management skills through formal training, which is by tradition highly regarded in China — there is a positive value in the concept of training as such. To get theoretical knowledge about the different leadership styles required for so-called situational leadership is often an eye opener. It can at first be hard to realize that depending on the situation and the person, I must choose different leadership styles.

12.4. Managing in Downturns

As we have seen, most businesses in China have had the advantage of living in a rapidly growing economy. Neither the Asian crisis in the second half of the 1990s nor the dotcom bust around the year 2000 really affected China that much. Dealing with a business downturn is new territory for local managers.

Employees are used to annual pay increases of 10% or more and to getting monthly calls from headhunters. Suddenly you learn that there will be no pay increase this year, your headhunters stop calling and some of your friends lose their jobs. People become worried.

Successful managers address these issues through communication, being proactive and sticking to a long-term strategy. During the financial crisis of 2008 and 2009, the following actions were successful:

- If they could, companies retained headcount by cutting other costs. China will continue to be a high-growth market long term. You will need the people, as well as their loyalty, when the market returns to normal.
- Companies ramped up internal communications functions to ensure that coworkers were kept informed of communicating and coaching coworkers to stress that what is now will not last forever.
- Companies put in place targeted sales efforts, taking into account the changed purchasing environment. In a downturn, existing customers buy less; the only way to maintain a healthy business is to find new customers.

Focused efforts usually give the best results, and allow the organization to concentrate on positive action.

Downturn Sales Team Focus

Some companies successfully applied the following approach to generate new customer leads.

In a downturn, existing customers buy less. It is therefore relatively easy to persuade your salespeople they do not need to spend as much time as usual selling to existing customers. Let us say you can liberate about 20%, or one full day per week.

In order to ensure that this "free time" is used chasing new customers, specific steps must be taken. One way is to set a schedule where each sales person spends one full day a week exclusively on finding new customers. This takes some discipline; sales people tend to revert to familiar patterns of calling customers that they already know and are comfortable with. In order to avoid the time being siphoned off, efforts should be concentrated to the same workday every week, and each sales person must provide a (simple) written report on how the time was used, as well as the immediate results and follow-up activities for next week.

Chapter 13

Dealing with Head Office

There are many misunderstandings and myths about China; country, market, business environment, and in particular challenges such as cultural and economic differences. Most head office colleagues simply lack more than the most superficial understanding of the reality in which local management has to work. The successful local manager must manage expectations, ensure support, and communicate well with head office.

> Sometimes, you just do not know where to start explaining to headquarters, or foreign customers, why things are not working the way they should be. Johan remembers once receiving a call from a stressed-out and upset client complaining that it was impossible to get through to Eastwei's Shanghai office on the phone. Johan called the Shanghai office and, sure enough, he could not get through. When he called the head of the Shanghai office on his mobile, the exasperated manager explained that "yes, it is a problem, because yesterday night the rats seem to have eaten our switchboard". This was, at the time, not something Johan felt compelled to relay to the client.

13.1. Managing Expectations

In the 1980s, companies would come to China as part of their global strategy. "If we want to continue being the number one company in our industry worldwide, we need to be number one in

China" would be a typical comment from the Chairman of the Board of a global Fortune-500 company. As companies stumbled over failed joint-venture strategies with local partners whose ultimate objectives were quite different from those of their "foreign friends", management at headquarters started demanding a more prudent approach.

Some companies, like Sandvik, took a different and more careful approach, when establishing themselves in China. Starting with and operating a low-risk representative office for nearly 10 years (from 1985) in order to learn and to build a small business as a solid foundation, the company then started to look at different alternatives for establishing themselves more firmly in China. We looked at the possibilities of joint ventures, which then (in the early 1990s) were the normal way for a foreign company to establish themselves more firmly in China. The company's top management, however, was worried about the risk that the technology would be transferred to and used by the local partner. "Remember, no joint ventures. We must protect out technology" were the phrases used. Based on that Sandvik started its own company, the first Swedish wholly owned foreign investment in China.

In the 21st century, few companies accept a Chinese subsidiary that indefinitely drains resources from the global operations. These days, the demand is to make money in China. In other words, global management tends to demand the maximum growth attainable while maintaining acceptable profitability. "Acceptable profitability" in China should, as we see it, in most industries today be about the average of those of the company globally, perhaps allowing for a percent or two lower in order to finance fast local growth. There is generally no reason to allow the China operation to dilute shareholder value.

On the other hand, profitability targets must not be set too high. Placing inordinate demands on the profitability of the local organization can stump growth and force pricing structures that opens the playing field to competitors.

13.2. Ensuring Support

We have talked at length about the importance of long-term, top-heavy investment in China, in order to build a strong corporate culture and a sustainable business. Because these needs are so important, it is better to overestimate the investment and commitment necessary for success.

To build a strong China business, head office management must be committed to providing not only financial resources, but also management time, coaching, and training. Some of the things you should consider getting head office to commit to are:

- Senior manager visits to train local colleagues and to inculcate corporate culture, global work approaches, and values.
- Training programs abroad for local managers.
- Active involvement and ongoing feedback on developments from head office management; do not wait with getting them involved until you have a problem.

Such support should be explicit and quantified, and, when necessary, budgeted for.

13.3. Communicating and Educating

In our opinion, most managers of MNC's under-invest in keeping head office informed. The turnaround often comes in times of crisis, when HQ questions local activities. This can happen as a result of a scandal or media attention, because financial returns become lower, or for a number of other reasons. But at such times, trying to "explain China" to management can look like an excuse for local management failure.

Successful local managers have used the following approaches to keeping head office in the loop:

- Regular "letter from China" to top management, commenting on local issues and developments; this should go beyond the normal management reports, and can be distributed more widely than to one's own direct manager.

- Taking the opportunity to present China from a wider perspective when visiting head office or taking part in global management meetings.
- Chinese New Year gifts to top managers — perhaps a book about Chinese business or even culture to raise interest and understanding.
- Visitation programs, where local management actively invites different global functions to understand the local Chinese business environment. The best programs include speeches by external consultants and other experts, who often provide such services free of charge, seeing it as a marketing opportunity.
- Exchange programs, where the best local employees are given the opportunity to work at head office for a limited time, usually a few months. This is also a great training opportunity which ensures knowledge transfer from head office functions to local managers.